Google Web Toolkit 2 Application Development Cookbook

Over 70 simple but incredibly effective practical recipes to develop web applications using GWT with JPA, MySQL, and iReport

Shamsuddin Ahammad

[PACKT] open source*
PUBLISHING
community experience distilled

BIRMINGHAM - MUMBAI

Google Web Toolkit 2 Application Development Cookbook

First published: November 2010

Production Reference: 1191110

Published by Packt Publishing Ltd.
32 Lincoln Road
Olton
Birmingham, B27 6PA, UK.

ISBN 978-1-849512-00-8

www.packtpub.com

Cover Image by Vinayak Chittar (vinayak.chittar@gmail.com)

Credits

Author

Shamsuddin Ahammad

Reviewers

Ventsislav Chochev

Yiwen Ng (Tony)

Jagmohan Purohit

Acquisition Editor

Dilip Venkatesh

Development Editor

Neha Mallik

Technical Editor

Krutika Katelia

Copy Editor

Neha Shetty

Indexer

Tejal Daruwale

Editorial Team Leader

Akshara Aware

Project Team Leader

Ashwin Shetty

Project Coordinator

Michelle Quadros

Proofreader

Clyde Jenkins

Graphics

Nilesh Mohite

Production Coordinator

Kruthika Bangera

Cover Work

Kruthika Bangera

About the Author

Shamsuddin Ahammad is a Senior Lecturer and the Course Coordinator at Daffodil Institute of IT, Bangladesh. He has been teaching Java, Programming Methods, and Database Systems since 2002. He has experience in supervising hundreds of academic projects. Shamsuddin has a Masters degree in Management Information Systems (MIS) from Daffodil International University, Dhaka. He obtained the B.Sc. (Hons) degree in Computing and Information Systems (CIS) from NCC Education Ltd, U.K. and London Metropolitan University in a joint program from the Daffodil Institute of IT. Prior to that, he has completed the IDCS & IADCS of NCC Education Ltd. He is an Additional Reviewer of Conference on Quality Engineering in Software Technology (CONQUEST) organized by the International Software Quality Institute (iSQI) in Germany. He is the author of the book titled *iReport 3.7*, published by Packt Publishing in March, 2010.

Extraordinary moral support from my respected parents, Md. Saidur Rahaman and Suriya Begum, is my greatest inspiration to write this book. My loving wife, Jesmin Rashid, has played a great role in my progression.

My brother and sisters, relatives, friends, and colleagues at Daffodil Institute of IT have inspired me a lot to writing this book—a special thanks to all of them. I'm very thankful to my teacher, Md. Nasimul Kader Sohel, for his warm support.

It is my great fortune to have worked with a great team of publishing professionals at Packt Publishing. I extend my sincerest gratitude to Dilip Venkatesh, Neha Mallik, Krutika Katelia and Michelle Quadros for their great cooperation in writing this book.

About the Reviewers

Ventsislav Chochev is software developer from Bulgaria, Europe. His educational degree is Bachelor of Informatics in "Computer programming and design". He currently works in IDxS, Belgium as a web developer, mainly using Java EE, Seam/Spring framework for their sensor's data presentation. His background covers many activities, such as using GWT and Java for application development.

Yiwen Ng (Tony) is a Java software developer with over seven years of commercial application development and consulting experience. Fringe passions involve agile methodology, mobile development, web enterprise development, configuration management, and security. If cornered, he may actually admit to knowing the latest technologies in Java and pair programming.

He's easily amused by programming language design and collaborative applications. Yiwen also develops a few android mobile applications and RIA GWT-based web applications. Occasionally, he works as a consultant on a contract basis. Yiwen may be reached directly via email at `ttony@mjsoft.com.au`.

Currently, he is employed at Tullett Prebon in Singapore as a Senior Software Developer.

Jagmohan Purohit started his career in MindTree Ltd. in 2007 as a Programmer Analyst. Over the course of his career, he had the good fortune of working on diverse technologies and vertical industries. He has over three years of experience in GWT and Smart GWT. Currently, he is playing the role of a Senior Software Engineer at MindTree Ltd. His current area of interest includes GWT, Alfresco, and Weblogic Portal.

His family hails from Berhampur in Orissa. He completed his graduation in Engineering from NIST (National Institute of Science and Technology), Berhampur in 2007. His other hobbies include travelling and reading.

> Reviewing GWT 2 Application Development Cookbook was a wonderful experience, which gave me an opportunity to know about Ext GWT integration and some best practices for GWT coding.

Table of Contents

Preface

GWT 2 radically improves the web experience for users by using the existing Java tools to build a no-compromise AJAX for any modern browser. It provides a solid platform so that the other great libraries can be built on top of the GWT. Creating web applications efficiently and making them impressive, however, is not as easy as it sounds. Writing web applications for multiple browsers can be quite tasking. In addition, building, reusing, and maintaining large JavaScript code bases and AJAX components can be difficult.

GWT 2 Application Development Cookbook eases these burdens by allowing the developers to build and maintain complex, yet highly efficient JavaScript frontend applications in the Java programming language quickly. It tells you how to make the web experience all the more thrilling and hassle-free by using various tools along with the GWT SDK.

This book starts with developing an application from scratch. Right from creating the layout of the home page to home page elements including left and right sidebars, to placing a tree-like navigational menu, menu bars, tool bars, banners, and footers are discussed with examples.

You will see how to create forms using the Ext GWT library widgets and handle different types of events. Then, you will move on to see how to design a database for sales processing systems, and learn how to create the database in MySQL with the help of easy-to-follow recipes.

One of the interesting topics of this book is using the JPA in GWT. Using the JPA object in GWT is a challenge. To use it perfectly, a mechanism to convert the JPA object into a plain object and vice versa is required. You will see recipes to use entity classes, entity managers, and controller classes in the GWT application. You will efficiently create reports with parameters, variables, and subreports, and get the report output in both HTML and PDF formats using real-world recipes.

You will then learn how to configure the GlassFish server to deploy a GWT application with a database. Finally, you will learn how to trace speed and improve performance in web applications using tracing techniques.

Create impressive web applications with tool bars, menus, multiple windows, and more with this step-by-step guide.

What this book covers

Chapter 1, Setting up the GWT Environment in NetBeans shows which tools and technologies are required to build a web application using GWT, JPA, and iReport in NetBeans. The required installation and configuration of the tools are shown as easy-to-follow recipes.

Chapter 2, Creating Home Page with Panels and Menus creates the layout of the application. It shows how to divide the page into the banner, left and right sidebars, and the center and footer sections.

Chapter 3, Forms with Layout and Widgets includes recipes that show how to use widgets to create forms, sidebars for navigation, tab panel, and so on.

Chapter 4, Handling your First Events includes easy-to-follow recipes that show how to handle the typical GWT events such as button event, field event, menu event, focus event, change event, and so on.

Chapter 5, Creating Database for Sales Processing creates a sample database in MySQL for Sales Processing Systems. To create a database and its tables with the required constraints, easily the uses of MySQL GUI tools have been shown.

Chapter 6, Managing Entities using JPA deals with the Java Persistence API (JPA) framework. It is a framework that is used to manage relational data in Java EE and Java SE applications. JPA provides a Plain Old Java Object (POJO) persistence model for object relational mapping. This chapter shows how to create a database connection, persistence unit, entity classes, and controller classes for the database CRUD operations.

Chapter 7, Communicating with Server using GWT RPC deals with the communication between the client and the server. The recipes in this chapter describe how to use the JPA in the server side and Data Transfer Objects (DTO) in the client side. It discusses how the GWT RPC mechanism allows the server and the client to pass Java objects back and forth.

Chapter 8, Reporting with iReport shows how to use iReport for the reporting solutions in Java web applications. Parameterized reports, subreports, and reports with variables are shown in some recipes. Then, the chapter discusses and shows how to show the created reports as HTML or PDF in the GWT application.

Chapter 9, Deploying a GWT Application includes recipes that show how to build the GWT project for the deployment, and before the deployment, how to create JDBC connection pool and resources in the GlassFish server are given as recipes.

Chapter 10, Using Speed Tracer deals with the extension Speed Tracer. Speed Tracer is a Google Chrome browser extension which is used to identify and fix performance problems in web applications. Installation and use of Speed Tracer for the created GWT applications are shown in this chapter.

What you need for this book

The software list required for this book is as follows:

Software	Download URL
JDK 6	http://www.oracle.com/technetwork/java/javase/downloads/index.html
GWT 2 SDK	http://code.google.com/webtoolkit/download.html
GlassFish 3.0.1	https://glassfish.dev.java.net/downloads/3.0.1-final.html
MySQL Community Server 5.1	http://www.mysql.com/downloads/mysql/
NetBeans	http://netbeans.org/downloads/index.html
GWT4NB	https://gwt4nb.dev.java.net/servlets/ProjectDocumentList
Ext GWT 2.2 SDK	http://www.sencha.com/products/gwt/thank-you.php?dl=extgwt220gwt2
iReport Plugin for NetBeans	http://jasperforge.org//website/ireportwebsite/IR%20Website/ir_download.html?header=project&target=ireport
Google Chrome	http://www.google.com/chrome
MySQL GUI tools	http://dev.mysql.com/downloads/gui-tools/5.0.html

Who this book is for

If you want to build AJAX web applications with GWT, then this book is for you. Developers with prior programming experience of Java development and object-oriented programming will find this book very useful.

Conventions

In this book, you will find a number of styles of text that distinguish between different kinds of information. Here are some examples of these styles, and an explanation of their meaning.

Code words in text are shown as follows: "We can include other contexts through the use of the `include` directive."

A block of code is set as follows:

```
menuBar.add(menuBarItemFile);
menuBar.add(menuBarItemReports);
menuBar.add(menuBarItemHelp);
```

New terms and important words are shown in bold. Words that you see on the screen, in menus or dialog boxes for example, appear in the text like this: "Right-click on the Servers option, and then click on Add Server."

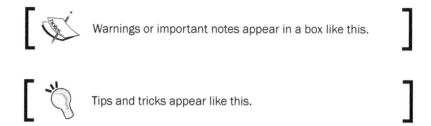

Warnings or important notes appear in a box like this.

Tips and tricks appear like this.

Reader feedback

Feedback from our readers is always welcome. Let us know what you think about this book—what you liked or may have disliked. Reader feedback is important for us to develop titles that you really get the most out of.

To send us general feedback, simply send an e-mail to `feedback@packtpub.com`, and mention the book title via the subject of your message.

If there is a book that you need and would like to see us publish, please send us a note in the SUGGEST A TITLE form on `www.packtpub.com` or e-mail `suggest@packtpub.com`.

If there is a topic that you have expertise in and you are interested in either writing or contributing to a book, see our author guide on `www.packtpub.com/authors`.

Customer support

Now that you are the proud owner of a Packt book, we have a number of things to help you to get the most from your purchase.

Downloading the example code for this book

You can download the example code files for all Packt books you have purchased from your account at `http://www.PacktPub.com`. If you purchased this book elsewhere, you can visit `http://www.PacktPub.com/support` and register to have the files e-mailed directly to you.

Errata

Although we have taken every care to ensure the accuracy of our content, mistakes do happen. If you find a mistake in one of our books—maybe a mistake in the text or the code—we would be grateful if you would report this to us. By doing so, you can save other readers from frustration and help us improve subsequent versions of this book. If you find any errata, please report them by visiting http://www.packtpub.com/support, selecting your book, clicking on the let us know link, and entering the details of your errata. Once your errata are verified, your submission will be accepted and the errata will be uploaded on our website, or added to any list of existing errata, under the Errata section of that title. Any existing errata can be viewed by selecting your title from http://www.packtpub.com/support.

Piracy

Piracy of copyright material on the Internet is an ongoing problem across all media. At Packt, we take the protection of our copyright and licenses very seriously. If you come across any illegal copies of our works, in any form, on the Internet, please provide us with the location address or website name immediately so that we can pursue a remedy.

Please contact us at copyright@packtpub.com with a link to the suspected pirated material.

We appreciate your help in protecting our authors, and our ability to bring you valuable content.

Questions

You can contact us at questions@packtpub.com if you are having a problem with any aspect of the book, and we will do our best to address it.

1
Setting up the GWT Environment in NetBeans

In this chapter, we will set up the required tools and technologies for developing an information system using the Google Web Toolkit (GWT). After that, we will create the GWT project in NetBeans IDE. The following recipes will be presented:

- ▸ Installing JDK
- ▸ Installing GWT SDK
- ▸ Installing GlassFish
- ▸ Installing MySQL Server
- ▸ Configuring the MySQL Server
- ▸ Installing NetBeans IDE
- ▸ Adding GlassFish Server in NetBeans
- ▸ Installing GWT4NB plugins in NetBeans
- ▸ Creating a GWT project in NetBeans
- ▸ Adding Ext GWT

Introduction

The main topic of the book is the Google Web Toolkit (GWT). However, GWT SDK alone is not enough to develop complete information systems. Some other tools and techniques have to be combined together to work with GWT. In this chapter, we will be introduced to some technologies and tools, get an overview of each, and set up all the required tools, technologies, and libraries. Here, JDK and GWT SDK are compulsory; the other tools have alternatives—we will cover these in this book.

Installing JDK

Because GWT is a Java-based development toolkit, Java SE Development Kit (JDK) must be installed for the development of a GWT project. We will use the NetBeans IDE, which also requires JDK to be installed.

Getting ready

Download the JDK, which is freely available from Sun Developer Networks (SDN) Downloads at `http://www.oracle.com/technetwork/indexes/downloads/index.html`.

How to do it...

1. Execute the JDK installer. For windows, the installer filename is `jdk-6u18-windows-i586.exe`, or something similar to this.

2. Accept the License Agreement.

3. Select the features to be installed from the given list. The available features are **Development Tools**, **Demos and Samples**, **Source Code**, **Public JRE**, and **Java DB**. **Java DB** is not required for our purpose.

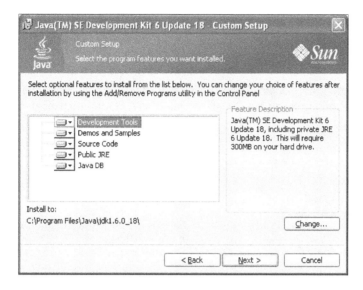

4. Set the installation directory.
5. Click on **Next** and follow the instructions.

Installing GWT SDK

The Google Web Toolkit (GWT) is an open source Java-based development toolkit for creating browser-based applications with a JavaScript frontend. GWT has made some tasks easier for the developers, as they do not need to have expertise in browser quirks, JavaScript, and scriptlets. Just by writing Java code, web-based GUIs like Swing can be developed using the GWT UI class library. The GWT SDK enables the developer to write the AJAX frontend in Java programming language, which is then converted to optimized JavaScript files that works in all the major browsers.

Important features

The following are some important features of GWT:

- The GWT can handle all of the client-server communications, whether it is JSON, XML, or GWT's Remote Procedure Call (RPC). Java objects can be passed between the client and the server
- A GWT application can communicate back and forth without having Java on the server because it works with standard communication protocols
- Pure object-oriented techniques can be used
- Allows HTML and JavaScript code, if required

- ▸ The GWT uses CSS for formatting
- ▸ IDE support is available from Eclipse, NetBeans, and IntelliJ IDEA
- ▸ It is free and open source

The GWT is used by many Google products, and thousands of other products around the world. Some real-world projects are Google Wave, Google Moderator, Google AdWords, Orkut, Gmail, Go Grid, Lombardi Blueprint, Scenechronize, Whirled, and so on.

GWT SDK contains the core libraries and a compiler that we need in order to develop GWT applications.

Getting ready

Go to `http://code.google.com/webtoolkit/download.html` and download the SDK. The SDK will be downloaded as a `ZIP` file named `gwt-2.0.3.zip` (or something similar to that).

How to do it...

Just extract the downloaded `ZIP` file to `C:\Program Files` or any desired directory of your choice.

Installing GlassFish

GlassFish is an open source Java EE-compatible application server. At the time of writing this book, the latest release of the server is version 3, which provides the fully-featured Java EE 6 and JPA reference implementation. GlassFish is based on the source code released by Sun and Oracle Corporation's TopLink persistence system. It is a fast, easy, and reliable application server.

The Java EE 6 platform significantly improves developer productivity, introduces the lightweight Web Profile for web-centric applications, and includes the latest versions of technologies, such as JavaServer Faces (JSF), Enterprise JavaBeans (EJB), Java Persistence API (JPA), Context and Dependency Injection (CDI), and many more.

 Please note that the other lightweight application servers, such as Tomcat or Jetty are also sufficient to run on it.

Getting ready

Download the GlassFish server installer from `http://developers.sun.com/appserver/downloads/index.jsp`.

How to do it...

1. Execute the GlassFish server installer `sges-v3-windows.exe` (Sun GlassFish Enterprise Server for Windows). It will extract the installation files, and then display the welcome screen:

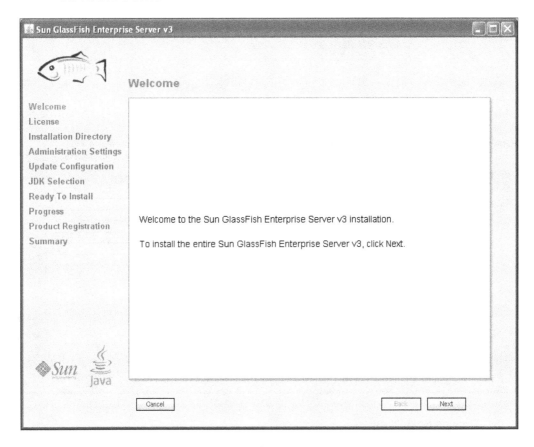

2. Click on **Next**.

3. Accept the terms, and then click on **Next**.

4. Specify the installation directory as `C:\Program Files\glassfishv3`, and then click on **Next**.

5. Configure the **Administration Settings** for **Admin Port**, **Http Port**, **Username**, and **Password**. The default values are 4848, 8080, and admin, respectively. Specify a password for the server.

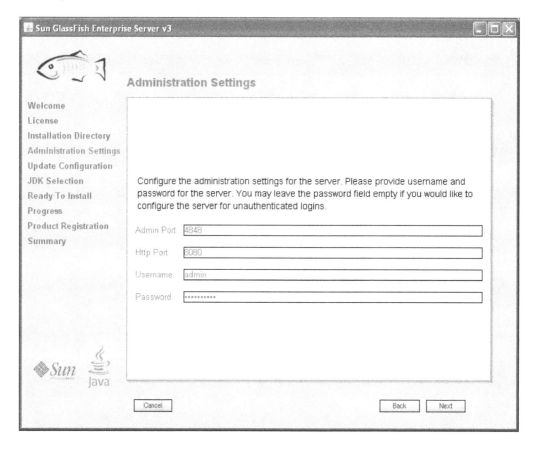

6. Click on **Next.**

7. Uncheck **Install Update Tool** and **Enable Update Tool** to set the **Update Configuration**.

8. Click on **Next.**

9. Select a **Java(TM) SDK** from the list. As we have already installed it, the list will automatically include **JDK 1.6.0_18**.

10. Click on **Next.**

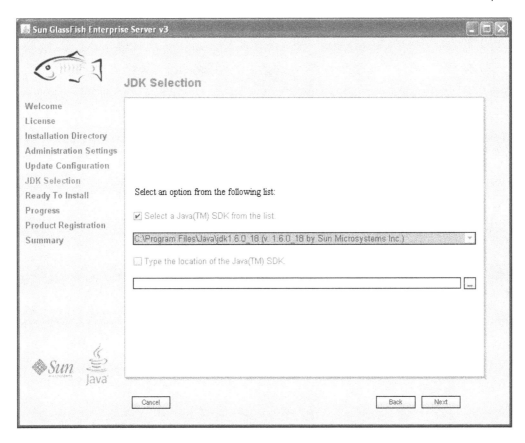

11. Click on **Install** and wait for the installation to complete. Skip **Product Registration**, which you can complete later.

12. Click on **Next**. It will show the installation summary, as shown in the following screenshot:

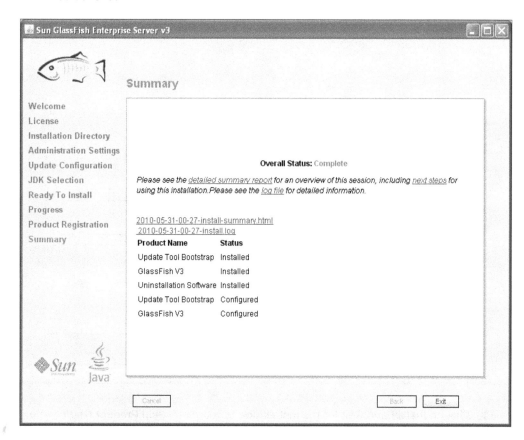

13. Click on **Exit**.

There's more...

We have seen here how to set up the GlassFish server from the standalone GlassFish installer. The GlassFish server is also bundled with the NetBeans installer. In that case, it is also possible to install the server during the installation of NetBeans IDE; a separate GlassFish installer will not be required.

See also

▶ Refer to the *Installing NetBeans IDE* recipe, later in the chapter

Installing MySQL server

MySQL is a relational database management system which runs as a server. MySQL server has a community edition freely available. In the perspective of this book, MySQL Community Server is picked to reside on the backend of the GWT application because some recipes are database-driven. It is worth mentioning here that the GWT does not require a database in all applications.

Getting ready

Download the MySQL Community Server from `http://dev.mysql.com/downloads/`. For Windows, the installer to be used is `mysql-essential-5.1.32-win32.msi`.

How to do it...

1. Execute the installer.
2. Click on **Next**.
3. Select **Complete** from the setup types.
4. Click on **Install** and wait until it finishes work.
5. Click on **Next**.
6. Click on **Next** again.
7. Uncheck **Configure the MySQL Server now**.
8. Click on **Finish** to complete the installation.

Configuring the MySQL Server

After installing the MySQL server, we need to configure the server instance.

Getting ready

If the MySQL server is not installed yet, install it first.

How to do it...

1. Go to **Start Menu | All Programs | MySQL | MySQL Server 5.1 | MySQL Server Instance Configuration Wizard**.

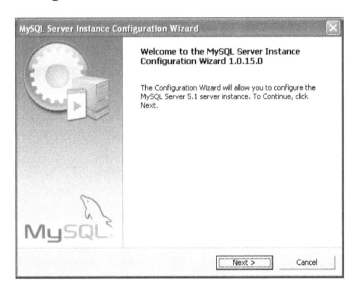

2. Click on **Next**.

3. Select **Standard Configuration** as the configuration type.

4. Click on **Next**.

5. Check **Install as Windows Service**, select **MySQL501** from the **Service Name** field, and check **Launch the MySQL Server automatically**.

6. Check **Include Bin Directory in Windows PATH**.

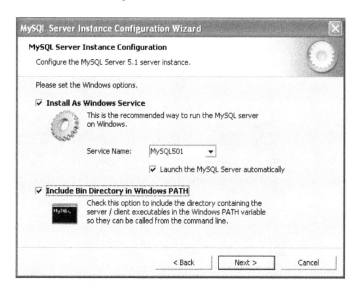

7. Click on **Next**.

8. Set the root password.

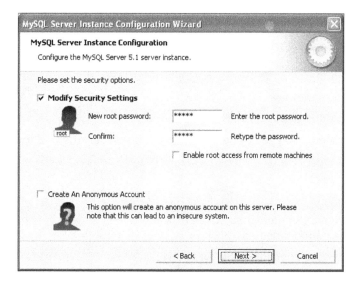

9. Click on **Next**.
10. Click on **Execute** to start the configuration.
11. After the configuration is processed, click on **Finish** to close the wizard.

Installing NetBeans IDE

The NetBeans project consists of an open source Integrated Development Environment (IDE) and an application platform, which enables building applications for web, desktop, or mobile. Applications can be built using Java, PHP, Python, Ruby, Groovy, C, C++, and so on.

This IDE is developed using Java and requires JVM to run.

Its important features are as follows:

- Web projects with Java EE 6
- EJBs support in web applications
- Java Persistence API deployment, debugging, and profiling with GlassFish v3 application server
- Database integration
- Java debugger
- Profiler support for monitoring Java applications to find memory leaks and for optimizing performance
- GUI design tools (not applicable for GWT yet)
- Extended support for JavaScript, AJAX, and CSS through NetBeans JavaScript Editor modules

Getting ready

Download the NetBeans IDE from `http://netbeans.org/downloads/index.html`.

How to do it...

1. Execute the installer `netbeans-6.8-ml-windows.exe` for installation on Windows.
2. Click on **Customize**.
3. Select **Base IDE**, **Java SE**, and **Java Web and EE**. Because we have already installed the GlassFish server separately, uncheck **Sun GlassFish Enterprise Server** and click on **OK**.

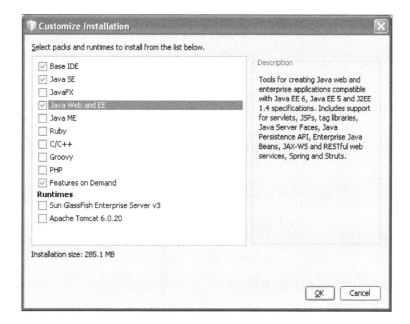

4. Click on **Next**.
5. Accept the terms, click on **Next**, and follow the instructions on the screen.
6. Click on **Finish** to complete the installation.

Adding the GlassFish server in NetBeans

We have installed the GlassFish server and the NetBeans IDE separately. Actually, we will start, stop, and deploy to the GlassFish server from NetBeans; that's why, we need to add the GlassFish Server in NetBeans. If the bundled version of NetBeans is used for installation, we do not need to add the server manually.

Getting ready

Make sure that both GlassFish and NetBeans are installed.

How to do it...

1. Start the NetBeans IDE.

2. Go to **Window | Services** to open the **Services** window:

3. Right-click the **Servers** option, and then click on **Add Server**:

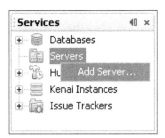

4. Choose **GlassFish v3** from the list:

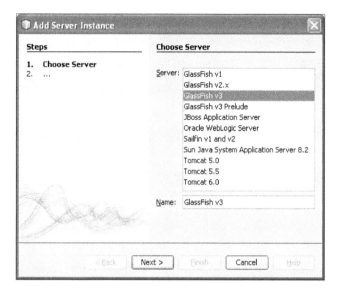

5. Click on **Next**.

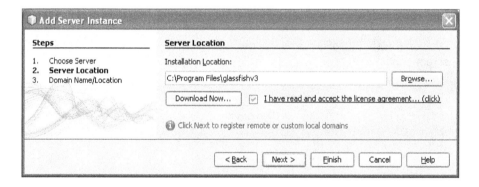

6. Browse the installation directory of the GlassFish server. In our case, it is `C:\ Program Files\glassfishv3`. Check the option **I have read and accept the license agreement**.

7. Click on **Next**.

8. Select **Register Local Domain** as the domain location, and **domain1** for the **Domain** field.

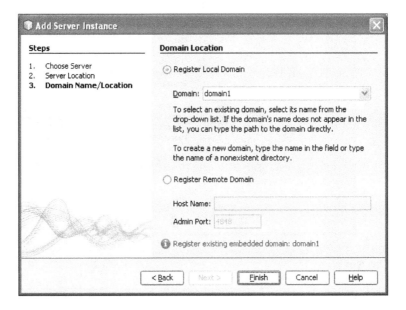

9. Click on **Finish**. GlassFish is now added under **Servers**, as seen in the following screenshot:

There's more...

Because we added the GlassFish server in NetBeans, the following server options are available, which can be accessed by right-clicking on **GlassFish v3** under **Servers**. Some of the options are as follows:

► **Start**
► **Restart**
► **Stop**

- **Refresh**
- **Remove**
- **View Admin Console**
- **View Server Log**
- **Properties**

Installing the GWT4NB plugin in NetBeans

GWT4NB is the only plugin so far for NetBeans IDE to develop web applications using the Google Web Toolkit.

Its features are as follows:

- Assistance in code editing for creating GWT EntryPoint, GWT RPC service, defining asynchronous methods, GWT modules, and so on
- Deployment, running, and debugging GWT applications from inside NetBeans

Getting ready

Download the latest version of GWT4NB from `https://gwt4nb.dev.java.net`. The filename is `org-netbeans-modules-gwt4nb.nbm`.

How to do it...

1. Start NetBeans.

2. Go to **Tools** | **Plugins** and click on the **Downloaded** tab.

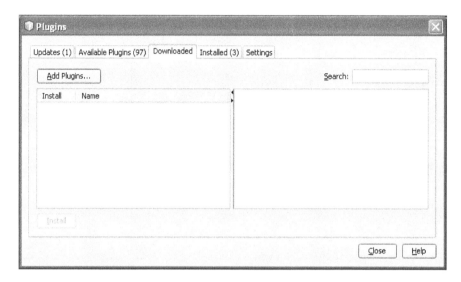

3. Click on the **Add Plugins...** button and open the **org-netbeans-modules-gwt4nb.nbm** file.

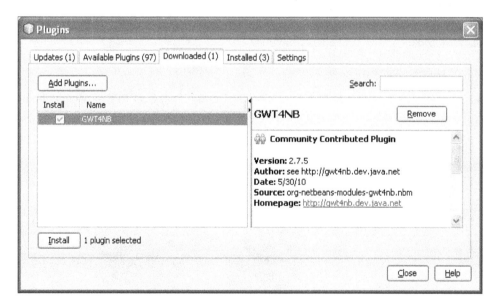

4. Click on **Install**.

5. Click on **Next**.

6. Accept the **License Agreement**.

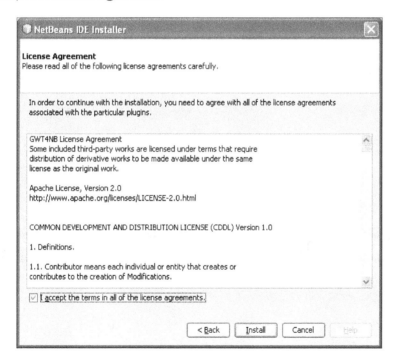

7. Click on **Install**.

8. Click on **Continue** when the **Validation Warning** window is displayed.

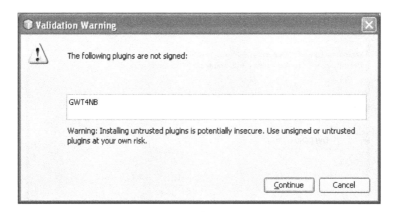

9. Wait for the installation to complete and then click on **Finish**.

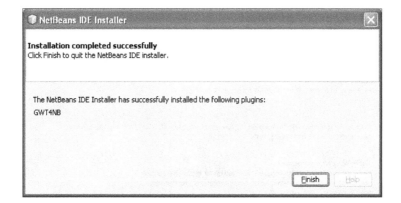

10. Close the plugins dialog.

Creating a GWT project in NetBeans

All the required tools and technologies are installed. Now, we will create the Java Web project using the Google Web Toolkit Framework in NetBeans.

Getting ready

Make sure that GWT and GlassFish are installed, the GlassFish server is added, and the GWT4NB plugin is installed in NetBeans.

How to do it...

1. Start NetBeans.

2. Go to **File | New Project**.

3. Select **Java Web** from the **Categories** field, and **Web Application** from the **Projects** field, as shown in the following screenshot:

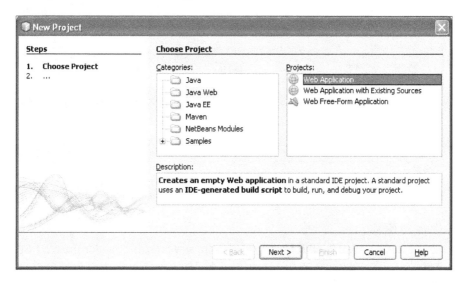

4. Click on **Next**.

5. Give **Sales Processing System** as the **Project Name**, browse the **Project Location**, and check **Set as Main Project**:

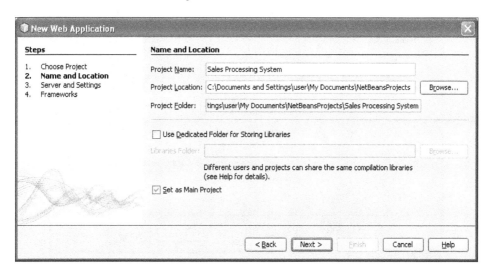

6. Click on **Next**.

7. Select **GlassFish v3** from the **Server** list, and **Java EE 6 Web** from the **Java EE Version**.

8. Set the **Context Path**, or leave it as suggested. It is the path to the "root directory" of a web application (called the context root), relative to the root of the web server namespace.

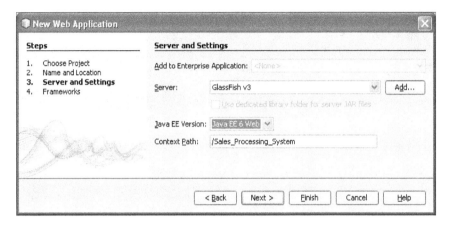

9. Click on **Next**.

10. Select **Google Web Toolkit** from the list of frameworks, browse for the GWT SDK Installation folder (such as `C:\Program Files\gwt-2.0.3`, or any other location where you have installed it), and name the GWT Module as `com.packtpub.Main`:

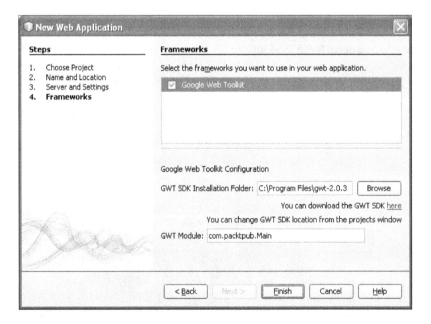

11. Click on **Finish** on completion of the installation.

How it works...

After following the aforementioned steps, a NetBeans project structure with some sections containing the following files has been created:

- ▶ Web Pages

  WEB-INF
    - ❏ sun-web.xml
    - ❏ web.xml

  welcomeGWT.html

- ▶ Source Packages

  com.packtpub
    - ❏ Main.gwt.xml

  com.packtpub.client
    - ❏ MainEntryPoint

- ▶ Libraries

  GWT2.0.3-gwt-user.jar

  gwt-dev.jar

  gwt-servlet.jar

  JDK1.6

  GlassFish v3

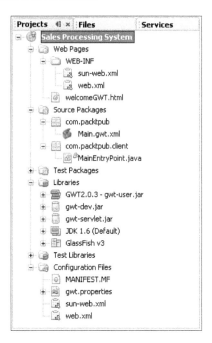

Directory and file structure

A directory and file structure is created, as shown in the following screenshot:

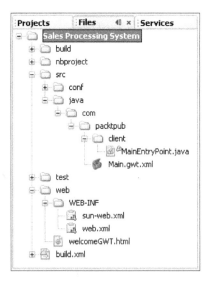

Running the project

A default code is given in the `MainEntryPoint.java` file. That's why, we can run the project to see a basic output. To run the project, right-click on **Sales Processing System** under **Projects** and then click on **Run**, as shown in the following screenshot:

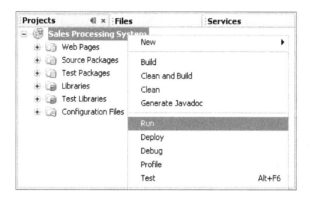

The following events take place:

1. GlassFish is started automatically, if it is not started yet. It will prompt the user for the username and password. Provide "admin" as the username and "adminadmin" as the password (or as we had set during the installation of GlassFish).

2. The project is compiled by GWT Compiler.

3. The project is deployed to the `\Sales Processing System\build\web` directory.

4. The default browser is called with the URL `http://localhost:8080/Sales_Processing_System/`.

5. The output is a button labeled **Click me!**. If the button is clicked, a label, **Hello, GWT!!!**, is hidden and displayed alternately:

Adding Ext GWT

Ext GWT is a Java UI component library developed by Ext JS, Inc. for building rich web applications with the Google Web Toolkit.

Its important features include the following:

▸ High performance, customizable UI components, panels, windows, menus, and so on

▸ Standard CSS support

▸ Well-documented source code

▸ Native GWT solution without any external JavaScript or third-party libraries

▸ Full remote procedure support using GWT RPC, JSON, and XML

▸ Support for Java 1.5 features, including generics, enums, and varargs

▸ Commercial and open source licenses available

Getting ready

Download Ext GWT SDK from `http://www.sencha.com/products/gwt/download.php`.

The file `gxt-2.1.1-gwt2.zip` is the EXT GWT 2.1.1 PUBLIC RELEASE for GWT 2.

How to do it...

1. Extract `gxt-2.1.1-gwt2.zip` to `C:\Program Files\` or any other desired location.

2. The next step is to add the Ext GWT library in the Sales Processing System project. To do this:

   ❑ Right-click on **Libraries** under the **Project** tab, and click on **Add Jar/Folder**

   ❑ Open the `gxt.jar` file from `C:\Program Files\gxt-2.1.1-gwt2\gxt-2.1.1`(or from the location to which the file was extracted), as shown in the following three screenshots:

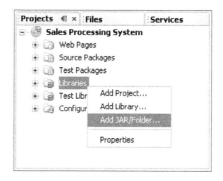

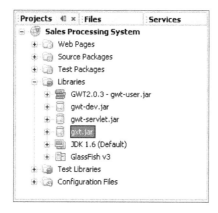

3. The next step is to place the Ext GWT `resources` folder containing the CSS, images, and others into the `web` folder of the `Sales Processing System` project.

   ❏ Copy the folder **resources** from `C:\Program Files\gxt-2.1.1-gwt2\` `gxt-2.1.1`(or from the location to which the file was extracted)

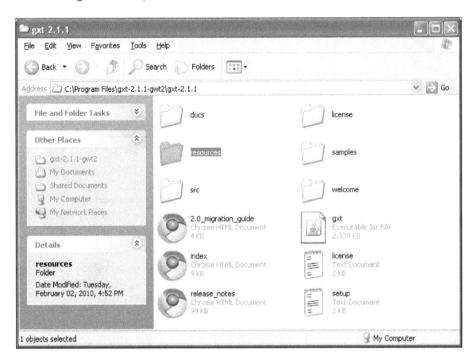

4. Paste it in the **web** folder by going to the **Files** tab, as shown in the following screenshot:

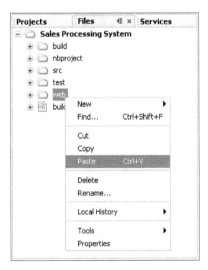

5. Now, we need to modify the GWT module:

   ❑ Open `Main.gwt.xml` from **Source Packages | com.packtpub**

   ❑ Expand the **General** node:

   ❑ Click on **Add** and write the module name `com.extjs.gxt.ui.GXT`:

   ❑ Save and close `Main.gwt.xml`

   ❑ Modify `welcomeGWT.html` to add a link to the CSS in the `/web/resources/css` folder

   ❑ Open `welcomeGWT.html`

   ❑ Add the following line just above the `</head>` tag:

```
<link rel="stylesheet" type="text/css"
   href="resources/css/gxt-all.css" />
```

Now, we are ready to start developing the GWT application

How it works...

Let's explain how these steps allow us to complete the task or solve the problem.

Adding the GXT JAR file allows us to use the widget library to create the user interfaces. Some important widgets used in this book from this library are Grids, Panels, Tabs, Layouts, Forms, Toolbar, Menu bar, Fields, Buttons, and so on.

The resources folder in the GXT contains the required CSS used in the widget library, images, and so on. By placing this folder in our application, we are being able to create nice user interfaces even without using any new CSS or images, though we can do so if required.

See also

▶ *Google Web Toolkit Overview*, available at `http://code.google.com/webtoolkit/overview.html`

▶ *Google Web Toolkit (GWT)*, by Mark Volkmann, available at `http://java.ociweb.com/mark/other-presentations/GWT.pdf`

▶ *Google Web Toolkit*, available at `http://en.wikipedia.org/wiki/Google_Web_Toolkit`

▶ *GlassFish Wiki*, available at `http://wiki.glassfish.java.net`

▶ *About MySQL*, available at `http://www.mysql.com/about`

▶ *NetBeans IDE 6.8 Release Information*, available at `http://netbeans.org/community/releases/68`

▶ *GWT4NB*, available at `https://gwt4nb.dev.java.net`

▶ *Ext GWT*, available at `http://www.sencha.com/products/gwt/`

2
Creating Home Page with Panels and Menus

In this chapter, we will cover:

- ▶ Creating the home page layout class
- ▶ Adding the banner
- ▶ Adding menus
- ▶ Creating the left-hand sidebar
- ▶ Creating the right-hand sidebar
- ▶ Creating the main content panel
- ▶ Creating the footer
- ▶ Using `HomePage` instance in `EntryPoint`

Introduction

In this chapter, we will learn about creating the home page of our application. The home page will include a banner at the top, a sidebar for navigation on the left-hand side, another sidebar on the right-hand side for showing dynamic content, a footer to show copyright and other information, and the main content at the center.

The layout will be as shown in the diagram below:

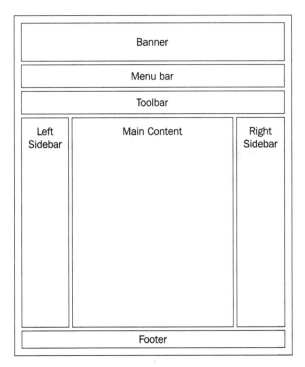

Creating the home page layout class

This recipe creates a panel to place the menu bar, banner, sidebars, footer, and the main application layout. Ext GWT provides several options to define the top-level layout of the application. We will use the `BorderLayout` function. We will add the actual widgets after the layout is fully defined. The other recipes add the menu bar, banner, sidebars, and footers each, one-by-one.

Getting ready

Open the **Sales Processing System** project.

How to do it...

Let's list the steps required to complete the task.

1. Go to **File | New File**.
2. Select **Java** from **Categories**, and **Java Class** from **File Types**.

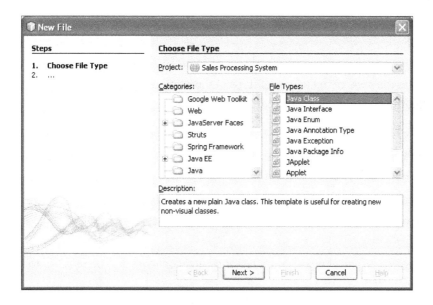

3. Click on **Next**.

4. Enter **HomePage** as the **Class Name**, and **com.packtpub.client** as **Package**.

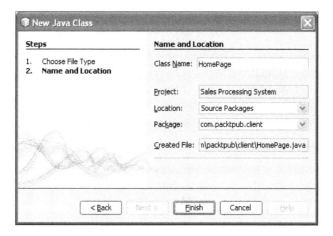

5. Click on **Finish**.

6. Inherit the class `ContentPanel`. Press *Ctrl + Shift + I* to import the package automatically. Add a default constructor:

```java
package com.packtpub.client;
import com.extjs.gxt.ui.client.widget.ContentPanel;
public class HomePage extends ContentPanel
{
  public HomePage()
```

```
    {

    }
}
```

Write the code of the following steps in this constructor.

7. Set the size in pixels for the content panel:

    ```
    setSize(980,630);
    ```

8. Hide the header:

    ```
    setHeaderVisible(false);
    ```

9. Create a `BorderLayout` instance and set it for the content panel:

    ```
    BorderLayout layout = new BorderLayout();
    setLayout(layout);
    ```

10. Create a `BorderLayoutData` instance and configure it to be used for the menu bar and toolbar:

    ```
    BorderLayoutData menuBarToolBarLayoutData=
        new BorderLayoutData(LayoutRegion.NORTH, 55);
    menuBarToolBarLayoutData.setMargins(new Margins(5));
    ```

11. Create a `BorderLayoutData` instance and configure it to be used for the left-hand sidebar:

    ```
    BorderLayoutData leftSidebarLayoutData =
        new BorderLayoutData(LayoutRegion.WEST, 150);
    leftSidebarLayoutData.setSplit(true);
    leftSidebarLayoutData.setCollapsible(true);
    leftSidebarLayoutData.setMargins(new Margins(0, 5, 0, 5));
    ```

12. Create a `BorderLayoutData` instance and configure it to be used for the main contents, at the center:

    ```
    BorderLayoutData mainContentsLayoutData =
        new BorderLayoutData(LayoutRegion.CENTER);
    mainContentsLayoutData.setMargins(new Margins(0));
    ```

13. Create a `BorderLayoutData` instance and configure it to be used for the right-hand sidebar:

    ```
    BorderLayoutData rightSidebarLayoutData =
        new BorderLayoutData(LayoutRegion.EAST, 150);
    rightSidebarLayoutData.setSplit(true);
    rightSidebarLayoutData.setCollapsible(true);
    rightSidebarLayoutData.setMargins(new Margins(0, 5, 0, 5));
    ```

14. Create a `BorderLayoutData` instance and configure it to be used for the footer:

```
BorderLayoutData footerLayoutData =
  new BorderLayoutData(LayoutRegion.SOUTH, 20);
footerLayoutData.setMargins(new Margins(5));
```

How it works...

Let's now learn how these steps allow us to complete the task of designing the application for the home page layout. The full page (home page) is actually a "content panel" that covers the entire area of the host page. The content panel is a container having top and bottom components along with separate header, footer, and body sections. Therefore, the content panel is a perfect building block for application-oriented user interfaces.

In this example, we will place the banner at the top of the content panel. The body section of the content panel is further subdivided into five regions in order to place these—the menu bar and toolbar at the top, two sidebars on each side, a footer at the bottom, and a large area at the center to place the contents like forms, reports, and so on. A `BorderLayout` instance lays out the container into five regions, namely, north, south, east, west, and center. By using `BorderLayout` as the layout of the content panel, we will get five places to add five components.

`BorderLayoutData` is used to specify layout parameters of each region of the container that has `BordeLayout` as the layout. We have created five instances of `BorderLayoutData`, to be used in the five regions of the container.

There's more...

Now, let's talk about some general information that is relevant to this recipe.

Setting the size of the panel

The `setSize` method is used to set the size for a panel. Any one of the two overloaded `setSize` methods can be used. A method has two `int` parameters, namely, width and height. The other one takes the same arguments as string.

Showing or hiding header in the content panel

Each content panel has built-in headers, which are visible by default. To hide the header, we can invoke the `setHeaderVisible` method, giving `false` as the argument, as shown in the preceding example.

BorderLayoutData

`BorderLayoutData` is used to set the layout parameters, such as margin, size, maximum size, minimum size, collapsibility, floatability, split bar, and so on for a region in a border panel.

Consider the following line of code in the example we just saw:

```
BorderLayoutData leftSidebarLayoutData =
  new BorderLayoutData(LayoutRegion.WEST, 150)
```

It creates a variable `leftSidebarLayoutData`, where the size is 150 pixels and the region is the west of the border panel.

`rightSidebarLayoutData.setSplit(true)` sets a split bar between this region and its neighbors. The split bar allows the user to resize the region.

`leftSidebarLayoutData.setCollapsible(true)` makes the component collapsible, that is, the user will be able to collapse and expand the region.

`leftSidebarLayoutData.setMargins(new Margins(0, 5, 0, 5))` sets a margin where 0, 5, 0, and 5 are the top, right, bottom, and left margins, respectively.

Classes and packages

In the preceding example, some classes are used from Ext GWT library, as shown in the following

Class	Package
BorderLayout	com.extjs.gxt.ui.client.widget.layout
BorderLayoutData	com.extjs.gxt.ui.client.widget.layout
ContentPanel	com.extjs.gxt.ui.client.widget
Margins	com.extjs.gxt.ui.client.util
Style	com.extjs.gxt.ui.client

See also

- The *Adding the banner* recipe
- The *Adding menus* recipe
- The *Creating the left-hand sidebar* recipe
- The *Creating the right-hand sidebar* recipe
- The *Creating the main content panel* recipe
- The *Creating the footer* recipe
- The *Using the HomePage instance in EntryPoint* recipe

Adding the banner

This recipe will create a method that we will use to add a banner in the content panel.

Getting ready

Place the banner image `banner.png` at the location `\web\resources\images`. You can use your own image or get it from the code sample provided for this book on the Packt Publishing website (`www.packtpub.com`).

How to do it...

1. Create the method `getBanner`:

```
public ContentPanel getBanner()
{
  ContentPanel bannerPanel = new ContentPanel();
  bannerPanel.setHeaderVisible(false);
  bannerPanel.add(new Image("resources/images/banner.png"));
    Image("resources/images/banner.png"));
  return bannerPanel;
}
```

2. Call the method `setTopComponent` of the `ContentPanel` class in the following constructor:

```
setTopComponent(getBanner());
```

How it works...

The method `getBanner()` creates an instance `bannerPanel` of type `ContentPanel`. The `bannerPanel` will just show the image from the location `resources/images/banner.png`. That's why, the header is made invisible by invoking `setHeaderVisible(false)`. Instance of the `com.google.gwt.user.client.ui.Image` class, which represents the banner image, is added in the `bannerPanel`.

In the default constructor of the `HomePage` class, the method `setTopComponent(getBanner())` is called to set the image as the top component of the content panel.

See also

▸ The *Creating the home page layout class* recipe

▸ The *Adding menus* recipe

▸ The *Creating the left-hand sidebar* recipe

▸ The *Creating the right-hand sidebar* recipe

▸ The *Creating main content panel* recipe

▸ The *Creating the footer* recipe

▸ The *Using the HomePage instance in EntryPoint* recipe

Adding menus

In this recipe, we will create a method `getMenuBar` that does the following:

▸ Creates a menu bar

▸ Creates menus

▸ Creates menu items

▸ Adds menu items in menus

▸ Adds menus in the menu bar

How to do it...

Write the method header `public MenuBar getMenuBar()`, and do the following in the method body. Finally, this method should be called in the constructor of the class `HomePage` to add the menu bar in the application.

1. Create an instance of `MenuBar`:

   ```
   MenuBar menuBar=new MenuBar();
   ```

2. Create instances of `Menu`:

   ```
   Menu fileMenu=new Menu();
   Menu reportsMenu=new Menu();
   Menu helpMenu=new Menu();
   ```

3. Create the menu items and add them in corresponding menus:

   ```
   //Items for File menu

   MenuItem productMenuItem=new MenuItem("Product");
   fileMenu.add(productMenuItem);

   MenuItem stockMenuItem=new MenuItem("Stock");
   ```

```
fileMenu.add(stockMenuItem);

MenuItem purchaseMenuItem=new MenuItem("Purchase");
fileMenu.add(purchaseMenuItem);

MenuItem salesMenuItem=new MenuItem("Sales");
fileMenu.add(salesMenuItem);

//Items for Reports menu

MenuItem productListMenuItem=new MenuItem("Product List");
reportsMenu.add(productListMenuItem);

MenuItem stockStatusMenuItem=new MenuItem("Stock Status");
reportsMenu.add(stockStatusMenuItem);

MenuItem purchaseDetailMenuItem=new MenuItem(
  "Purchase Detail");
reportsMenu.add(purchaseDetailMenuItem);

MenuItem salesDetailMenuItem=new MenuItem("Sales Detail");
reportsMenu.add(salesDetailMenuItem);

//Items for Help menu

MenuItem aboutMenuItem=new MenuItem("About");
helpMenu.add(aboutMenuItem);
```

4. Create the menu bar items:

```
MenuBarItem menuBarItemFile=new MenuBarItem("File",fileMenu);
MenuBarItem menuBarItemReports=
  new MenuBarItem("Reports",reportsMenu);
MenuBarItem menuBarItemHelp=
  new MenuBarItem("Help",helpMenu);
```

5. Add the menu bar items in menu bar:

```
menuBar.add(menuBarItemFile);
menuBar.add(menuBarItemReports);
menuBar.add(menuBarItemHelp);
```

6. Return the menu bar:

```
return menuBar;
```

How it works...

The menu bar containing all the required menus with menu items is created in the following ways:

1. MenuBar instance `menuBar` is created where the menu bar items will be added.

2. Three menus are created for `File`, `Reports`, and `Help`.

3. Menu items are created and added under corresponding menus.

4. Three instances of `MenuBarItem` are created for the three menus.

5. All of the menu bar items are added in the menu bar. Call this method in the `HomePage` constructor by writing `add(getMenuBar, menuBarToolBarLayoutData)`.

Class	Package
MenuBar	com.extjs.gxt.ui.client.widget.menu
Menu	com.extjs.gxt.ui.client.widget.menu
MenuItem	com.extjs.gxt.ui.client.widget.menu
MenuBarItem	com.extjs.gxt.ui.client.widget.menu

See also

▸ The *Creating the home page layout class* recipe

▸ The *Adding the banner* recipe

▸ The *Creating the left-hand sidebar* recipe

▸ The *Creating the right-hand sidebar* recipe

▸ The *Creating the main content panel* recipe

▸ The *Creating the footer* recipe

▸ The *Using the HomePage instance in EntryPoint* recipe

Creating the left-hand sidebar

In this recipe, we are going to create a sidebar to be placed on the left-hand side of the homepage. This sidebar will be used for navigation.

How to do it...

1. Define the method `getLeftSidebar`:

```
public ContentPanel getLeftSideBar()
{
  ContentPanel leftSidebarPanel = new ContentPanel();
  leftSidebarPanel.setHeading("Left Sidebar");
  return leftSidebarPanel;
}
```

2. Call the `add` method of class `ContentPanel` in the constructor to add the sidebar in the content panel:

```
add(getLeftSideBar(), leftSidebarLayoutData);
```

How it works...

The method `getLeftSideBar` creates a content panel instance and sets a heading **Left Sidebar**. This heading will be modified later.

The left-hand sidebar created by this method is added in the west region of the main content panel by invoking `add(getLeftSideBar(), leftSidebarLayoutData)` in the constructor.

See also

- ▸ The *Creating the home page layout class* recipe
- ▸ The *Adding the banner* recipe
- ▸ The *Adding menus* recipe
- ▸ The *Creating the right-hand sidebar* recipe
- ▸ The *Creating the main content panel* recipe
- ▸ The *Creating the footer* recipe
- ▸ The *Using the HomePage instance in EntryPoint* recipe

Creating the right-hand sidebar

In this recipe, we are going to create a sidebar to be placed on the right-hand side. This sidebar will be used for some dynamic contents based on the main contents at the center.

How to do it...

1. Define the method `getRightSidebar`:

```
public ContentPanel getRightSideBar()
{
  ContentPanel rightSidebarPanel = new ContentPanel();
  rightSidebarPanel.setHeading("Right" Sidebar");
  return rightSidebarPanel;
}
```

2. Call the add method of class `ContentPanel` in the constructor to add the sidebar in the content panel:

```
add(getRightSideBar(), rightSidebarLayoutData);
```

How it works...

The method `getRightSideBar` creates a content panel instance, and sets a heading **Right Sidebar**. This heading will be modified later.

The right-hand sidebar created by this method is added in the east region of the main content panel by invoking `add(getRightSideBar(), rightSidebarLayoutData)` in the constructor.

See also

- ▸ The *Creating the home page layout class* recipe
- ▸ The *Adding the banner* recipe
- ▸ The *Adding menus* recipe
- ▸ The *Creating the left-hand sidebar* recipe
- ▸ The *Creating the main content panel* recipe
- ▸ The *Creating the footer* recipe
- ▸ The *Using the HomePage instance in EntryPoint* recipe

Creating the main content panel

In this recipe, we are going to create the main content panel, to be placed at the center. All forms and reports will be shown in this panel.

How to do it...

1. Define the method `getMainContents`:

```
public ContentPanel getMainContents()
{
    ContentPanel mainContentsPanel = new ContentPanel();
    mainContentsPanel.setHeading("Main Contents");
    return mainContentsPanel;
}
```

2. Call the `add` method of the `ContentPanel` class in the constructor to add the sidebar in the content panel:

```
add(getMainContents(), mainContentsLayoutData);
```

How it works...

The method `getMainContents` creates a `ContentPanel` instance and sets a heading **Main Contents**. This heading will be modified later.

The content panel created by this method is added at the center of the home page content panel by invoking `add(getMainContents(), mainContentsLayoutData)` in the constructor.

See also

- ▸ The *Creating the home page layout class* recipe
- ▸ The *Adding the banner* recipe
- ▸ The *Adding menus* recipe
- ▸ The *Creating the left-hand sidebar* recipe
- ▸ The *Creating the right-hand sidebar* recipe
- ▸ The *Creating the footer* recipe
- ▸ The *Using the HomePage instance in EntryPoint* recipe

Creating the footer

We are going to create the footer to place at the bottom of the page.

How to do it...

Let's list the steps required to complete the task:

1. Define the method `getFooter`:

```
public VerticalPanel getFooter()
{
  VerticalPanel footerPanel = new VerticalPanel();
  footerPanel.setHorizontalAlignment
    (HasHorizontalAlignment.ALIGN_CENTER);
  Label label = new Label("Design by Shamsuddin Ahammad.
    Copyright © Packt Publishing.");
  footerPanel.add(label);

  return footerPanel;
}
```

2. Call the `add` method of class `ContentPanel` in the constructor to add the footer at the bottom of the content panel:

```
add(getFooter(), footerLayoutData);
```

How it works...

Method `getFooter()` creates an instance of `VerticalPanel`, which contains a `Label` instance with some text. The label will be shown at the center of the vertical panel, as its horizontal alignment is set to center.

VerticalPanel

`VerticalPanel` is a panel that lays out its children in a vertical single column. In this recipe, only a single instance of Label is added as the child in the panel; that's why the `VerticalPanel` is chosen here.

Setting alignment for VerticalPanel

Two methods, `setHorizontalAlignment` and `setVerticalAlignment`, are used for setting alignment for `VerticalPanel`. The first method takes values of `HasHorizontalAlignment.HorizontalAlignmentConstant` type as arguments. The available constants are:

- `HasHorizontalAlignment.ALIGN_CENTER`
- `HasHorizontalAlignment.ALIGN_DEFAULT`
- `HasHorizontalAlignment.ALIGN_LEFT`
- `HasHorizontalAlignment.ALIGN_RIGHT`

The `setVerticalAlignment` method takes values of `HasVerticalAlignment.VerticalAlignmentConstant` type as argument. The available options are:

- `HasVerticalAlignment.BOTTOM`
- `HasVerticalAlignment.MIDDLE`
- `HasVerticalAlignment.TOP`

Class	Package
`HasHorizontalAlignment`	`com.google.gwt.user.client.ui`
`VerticalPanel`	`com.google.gwt.user.client.ui`
`Label`	`com.extjs.gxt.ui.client.widget`

See also

- The *Creating the home page layout class* recipe
- The *Adding the banner* recipe
- The *Adding menus* recipe
- The *Creating the left-hand sidebar* recipe

- ▸ The *Creating the right-hand sidebar* recipe
- ▸ The *Creating the main content panel* recipe
- ▸ The *Using the HomePage instance in EntryPoint* recipe

Using the HomePage instance in EntryPoint

To see the output of the created home page layout, we must add the `HomePage` instance in the root panel at the entry point class.

Getting ready

Open the file `MainEntryPoint.java`.

How to do it...

1. Remove all previous code from the method `onModuleLoad`:
2. Create an instance of the `HomePage` class in this method:

   ```
   HomePage homePage=new HomePage();
   ```

3. Add the `homepage` instance in the `RootPanel`:

   ```
   RootPanel.get().add(homePage);
   ```

How it works...

After adding the `HomePage` instance in the `RootPanel`, if we run the project, we will get the following output:

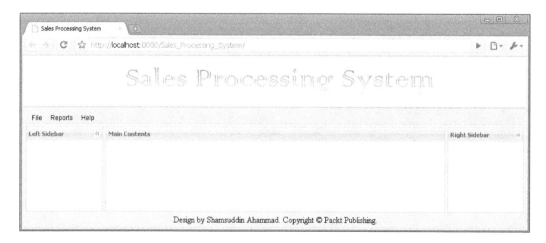

EntryPoint

EntryPoint is an interface that allows a class to act as a module entry point. When a module is loaded, each entry point class listed in the Main.gwt.xml file is instantiated and its onModuleLoad method is called. When the host page is accessed by the browser, the onModuleLoad function is called to display the first panels and widgets.

RootPanel

RootPanel corresponds to an HTML element on the host page. It can be used to add other panels and widgets. A RootPanel is accessed by calling RootPanel.get(id), where id is the value of the HTML ID attribute. The <body> element of the host page can be accessed by calling RootPanel.get().

 RootPanels are never created directly. Instead, they are accessed via get().

Class and packages

The following table shows the class and its corresponding package

Class	Package
EntryPoint	com.google.gwt.core.client
RootPanel	com.google.gwt.user.client.ui

See also

▶ The *Creating the home page layout class* recipe

▶ The *Adding the banner* recipe

▶ The *Adding menus* recipe

▶ The *Creating the left-hand sidebar* recipe

▶ The *Creating the right-hand sidebar* recipe

▶ The *Creating the main content panel* recipe

▶ The *Creating the footer* recipe

3
Forms with Layout and Widgets

In this chapter, we will cover:

- ▶ Using widgets
- ▶ Using TextField
- ▶ Using a simple combo box
- ▶ Using the radio button
- ▶ Using DateField
- ▶ Creating a simple form
- ▶ Creating a form with two columns
- ▶ Creating TabPanel to show forms as tabs
- ▶ Creating a navigation sidebar with Accordion layout

Introduction

In this chapter, we will create a Graphical User Interface (GUI) for accepting the user input and displaying information to the user. Using various types of widgets, we will create the necessary forms for the Sales Processing System project.

Using widgets

A widget is an element of the Graphical User Interface that displays information and is used for interaction with the user. Widgets are the visual building blocks for a GUI application. Many useful widgets are available in the Ext GWT library. Some of the common widgets are label, text field, button, combo box, check box, radio button, date picker, and so on, which are used in forms.

How to do it...

Using a widget in a form is very easy. For most widgets, the steps are as follows:

1. Create instances of the widget class. For example:

    ```
    CheckBox checkbox = new CheckBox();
    ComboBox comboBox = new ComboBox();
    DateField dateField = new DateField();
    Radio radio = new Radio();
    TextArea textArea = new TextArea();
    TextField textField = new TextField();
    ```

2. Set some properties for the widgets. For example, for a text field:

    ```
    textField.setFieldLabel("Name");
    textField.setAllowBlank(false);
    ```

3. Add the widget on the form or panel. For example:

    ```
    FormPanel formPanel=new FormPanel();
    formPanel.add(textField);
    ```

Using TextField

A text field allows the user to input one-line text information to the program. It is one of the most common widgets.

How to do it...

1. Import the class `com.extjs.gxt.ui.client.widget.form.TextField` from the GXT library.

2. Instantiate it as shown:

    ```
    TextField<String> nameField = new TextField<String>();
    ```

3. Set the required properties. Some examples are as follows:

    ```
    nameField.setAllowBlank(false);
    nameField.setEmptyText("Enter Employee's Full Name");
    nameField.setFieldLabel("Full Name");
    nameField.setSelectOnFocus(true);
    ```

4. Add the field on the required form or panel.

How it works...

Instantiating `TextField` with a `String` type parameter (within angle bracket as in `<String>`) allows the user to set and get the value of the `TextField` as `String`. If `Integer` is given as the parameter type, the `setValue` method of `TextField` will accept an `Integer` value as the argument, and the `getValue` method will return an `Integer` value.

The `setAllowBlank` method is used to set whether the field is valid when its value length is 0 (zero). Giving `false` as the argument means that it is a mandatory field and that the user must give an input; otherwise, an error will be indicated in the UI. On the other hand, giving `true` as the argument makes the field optional for input.

When there is no value in `TextField`, an empty text with a light foreground (most often light gray) is shown in the `TextField` by invoking the `setEmptyText` method with the message given as an argument.

To create a label for the `TextField`, the `setFieldLabel` method is used.

When the `TextField` gains focus, the existing value in `TextField` is automatically selected if the `setSelectOnFocus` method is called with `true` as the argument.

There's more...

`TextField` has some other special uses that are stated in the following sections.

Using TextField for password

To use `TextField` to accept a password, invoke the `setPassword(Boolean)` method. The password field is masked with stars, dots, or any other character. An example code is as follows:

```
TextField passwordField=new TextField();
passwordField.setPassword(true);
```

Creating a read-only TextField

Invoking the method `setReadOnly` with the argument `true` makes a text field read-only, that is, makes it non-editable.

Using a simple combo box

A combo box is a combination of a drop-down list and a text field. It allows the user to either select an item from the drop-down list or type a value directly. In this recipe, we are going to create a simple combo box for the department list.

How to do it...

1. Import the class `com.extjs.gxt.ui.client.widget.form.SimpleComboBox`.

2. Create an instance of `SimpleComboBox` class, as shown in the following code:

   ```
   SimpleComboBox departmentCombo = new SimpleComboBox();
   ```

3. Add values for the drop-down list as in the following code:

   ```
   departmentCombo.add("Sales");
   departmentCombo.add("Purchase");
   departmentCombo.add("Accounts");
   departmentCombo.add("Customer Service");
   ```

4. Set the field label and add the combo box on any form, panel, or relevant widget.

How it works...

Each invoke of the `add` method with an object as the argument (`String` object in this case) adds a value to the drop-down list of the combo box. Two methods—`setSimpleValue` and `getSimpleValue` are used to select a value programmatically and get the selected value respectively. These methods are most popular as getters and setters.

Using the radio button

The radio button is used when there are some predefined options from which only a single option is selected for a field. In this recipe, we are going to create radio buttons to use as options for the gender of a person. A radio group is a group of radio buttons which allows selecting only a single radio in the group.

How to do it...

1. Import the class `com.extjs.gxt.ui.client.widget.form.Radio`.

2. Create an instance for each of the options as shown:

   ```
   Radio maleRadio = new Radio();
   Radio femaleRadio = new Radio();
   ```

3. Set a label for each instance appearing beside the radio. The code for the same is as below:

   ```
   maleRadio.setBoxLabel("Male");
   femaleRadio.setBoxLabel("Female");
   ```

4. Create a `RadioGroup` instance:

   ```
   RadioGroup genderGroup = new RadioGroup();
   ```

5. Set a label for `RadioGroup` as shown:

```
genderGroup.setFieldLabel("Gender");
```

6. Add all the radio instances in the `RadioGroup` instance:

```
genderGroup.add(maleRadio);
genderGroup.add(femaleRadio);
```

7. Add the radio group in the required form, panel, or widget.

Using DateField

A calendar widget and a text field combined into the `DateField` widget allows to input date-type data. This calendar widget has more control of the date ranges. We can disable all the dates before a particular date, disable future dates, and so on. Keyboard navigation is also supported. In this recipe, we are going to create a `DateField` instance for the date of birth of a person.

How to do it...

1. Import the class `com.extjs.gxt.ui.client.widget.form.DateField`.

2. Create an instance of the `DateField` class as shown:

```
DateField dateOfBirthField = new DateField();
```

3. Set the minimum and maximum allowable date:

```
dateOfBirthField.setMinValue(new Date(80,1,1));
dateOfBirthField.setMaxValue(new Date());
```

4. Add the `DateField` instance to any form, panel, or relevant widget.

How it works...

In this recipe, the minimum and maximum dates are set respectively as January 1, 1980 and the current date. Any date before the minimum and after the maximum is not allowed to be selected.

Creating a simple form

In this recipe, we are going to create a simple form for adding, updating, deleting, and finding a branch in the Sales Processing System project.

How to do it...

1. Import the following classes:

```
import com.extjs.gxt.ui.client.widget.button.Button;
import com.extjs.gxt.ui.client.widget.form.FormPanel;
import com.extjs.gxt.ui.client.widget.form.TextField;
```

2. Create the `BranchForm` class that inherits the `FormPanel` class:

```
public class BranchForm extends FormPanel
```

3. Create the widget instances, as in the following code:

```
TextField<Integer> branchIdField = new TextField<Integer>();
TextField<String> nameField = new TextField<String>();
TextField<String> locationField = new TextField<String>();
Button findButton=new Button("Find");
Button saveButton=new Button("Save");
Button deleteButton=new Button("Delete");
Button clearButton=new Button("Clear");
```

4. Define the method `createForm` that sets the properties for the widgets and adds them, as in the following code:

```
private void createForm()
{
  branchIdField.setFieldLabel("Branch ID");
  branchIdField.setEmptyText("Enter the branch ID");
  branchIdField.setAllowBlank(false);

  nameField.setFieldLabel("Name");
  nameField.setEmptyText("Enter the branch name");
  nameField.setAllowBlank(false);

  locationField.setFieldLabel("Location");
  locationField.setEmptyText("Enter the branch location");
  locationField.setAllowBlank(true);

  add(branchIdField);
  add(nameField);
  add(locationField);

  addButton(findButton);
  addButton(saveButton);
  addButton(deleteButton);
  addButton(clearButton);
}
```

5. Define the constructor as shown:

```
public BranchForm()
{
    setHeading("Branch");
    setFrame(true);
    setSize(350,200);
    createForm();
}
```

6. Instantiate and add `BranchForm` to any form, panel, or relevant widget.

How it works...

By inheriting the `FormPanel` class, this class gets the characteristics of a form. The `createForm` method set labels and some other properties for the text fields, and adds the text fields and buttons in the form. If this class is instantiated and added, the following output will be seen:

Creating a form with two columns

In this recipe, we are going two create a form with two columns, as shown in the following screenshot:

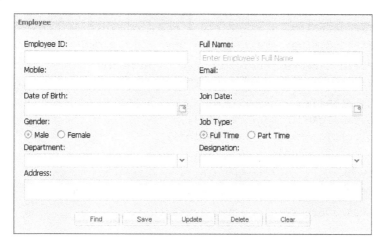

This form will be used to find, save, update, and delete employee information in the Sales Processing System project.

How to do it...

1. Import the following classes:

```
import com.extjs.gxt.ui.client.Style.HorizontalAlignment;
import com.extjs.gxt.ui.client.widget.LayoutContainer;
import com.extjs.gxt.ui.client.widget.button.Button;
import com.extjs.gxt.ui.client.widget.form.DateField;
import com.extjs.gxt.ui.client.widget.form.FormPanel;
import com.extjs.gxt.ui.client.widget.form.Radio;
import com.extjs.gxt.ui.client.widget.form.RadioGroup;
import com.extjs.gxt.ui.client.widget.form.SimpleComboBox;
import com.extjs.gxt.ui.client.widget.form.TextArea;
import com.extjs.gxt.ui.client.widget.form.TextField;
import com.extjs.gxt.ui.client.widget.layout.ColumnData;
import com.extjs.gxt.ui.client.widget.layout.ColumnLayout;
import com.extjs.gxt.ui.client.widget.layout.FormData;
import com.extjs.gxt.ui.client.widget.layout.FormLayout;
import java.util.Date;
```

2. Create the `EmployeeForm` class that inherits the `FormPanel` class:

```
public class EmployeeForm extends FormPanel
```

By inheriting the `FormPanel` class, the `EmployeeForm` class gets all properties of `FormPanel` class, which is a panel to display the form widgets.

3. Create the widget instances, as shown in the following code:

```
TextField<Integer> employeeIdField = new TextField<Integer>();
TextField<String> nameField = new TextField<String>();
TextField<String> mobileField = new TextField<String>();
TextField<String> emailField = new TextField<String>();

DateField dateOfBirthField = new DateField();
DateField joinDateField = new DateField();

Radio maleRadio = new Radio();
Radio femaleRadio = new Radio();
Radio fullTimeRadio = new Radio();
Radio partTimeRadio = new Radio();

SimpleComboBox departmentCombo = new SimpleComboBox();
SimpleComboBox designationCombo = new SimpleComboBox();

TextArea addressField = new TextArea();
```

```
Button findButton=new Button("Find");
Button saveButton=new Button("Save");
Button updateButton=new Button("Update");
Button deleteButton=new Button("Delete");
Button clearButton=new Button("Clear");
```

4. Define the method `createForm` that sets the properties for the widgets and adds them, as shown in the following code:

```
private void createForm()
{
  setFrame(true);
  setHeading("Employee");
  setSize(600, 500);
  setLabelAlign(LabelAlign.TOP);
  setButtonAlign(HorizontalAlignment.CENTER);
  LayoutContainer main = new LayoutContainer();
  main.setLayout(new ColumnLayout());

  LayoutContainer left = new LayoutContainer();
  left.setStyleAttribute("paddingRight", "10px");
  FormLayout layout = new FormLayout();
  layout.setLabelAlign(LabelAlign.TOP);
  left.setLayout(layout);

  FormData formData = new FormData("100%");

  employeeIdField.setFieldLabel("Employee ID");
  left.add(employeeIdField, formData);

  mobileField.setFieldLabel("Mobile");
  left.add(mobileField, formData);

  dateOfBirthField.setFieldLabel("Date of Birth");
  dateOfBirthField.setMinValue(new Date(80,1,1));
  dateOfBirthField.setMaxValue(new Date());
  left.add(dateOfBirthField, formData);

  maleRadio.setBoxLabel("Male");
  femaleRadio.setBoxLabel("Female");

  RadioGroup genderGroup = new RadioGroup();
  genderGroup.setFieldLabel("Gender");
  genderGroup.add(maleRadio);
  genderGroup.add(femaleRadio);
  left.add(genderGroup, formData);

  departmentCombo.setFieldLabel("Department");
  departmentCombo.add("Sales");
  departmentCombo.add("Purchase");
  departmentCombo.add("Accounts");
```

```
        departmentCombo.add("Customer Service");

        left.add(departmentCombo, formData);

        LayoutContainer right = new LayoutContainer();
        right.setStyleAttribute("paddingLeft", "10px");
        layout = new FormLayout();
        layout.setLabelAlign(LabelAlign.TOP);
        right.setLayout(layout);

        nameField.setAllowBlank(false);
        nameField.setEmptyText("Enter Employee's Full Name");
        nameField.setFieldLabel("Full Name");
        nameField.setSelectOnFocus(true);
        right.add(nameField, formData);

        emailField.setFieldLabel("Email");
        right.add(emailField, formData);

        joinDateField.setFieldLabel("Join Date");
        right.add(joinDateField, formData);

        fullTimeRadio.setBoxLabel("Full Time");
        partTimeRadio.setBoxLabel("Part Time");

        RadioGroup jobTypeGroup = new RadioGroup();
        jobTypeGroup.setFieldLabel("Job Type");
        jobTypeGroup.add(fullTimeRadio);
        jobTypeGroup.add(partTimeRadio);
        right.add(jobTypeGroup, formData);

        designationCombo.setFieldLabel("Designation");
        designationCombo.add("Manager");
        designationCombo.add("Officer");
        designationCombo.add("Salesman");
        designationCombo.add("Clerk");

        right.add(designationCombo, formData);

        main.add(left, new ColumnData(.5));
        main.add(right, new ColumnData(.5));

        add(main, new FormData("100%"));

        addressField.setFieldLabel("Address");
        addressField.setHeight(150);
        add(addressField, new FormData("100%"));

        addButton(findButton);
        addButton(saveButton);
        addButton(updateButton);
        addButton(deleteButton);
        addButton(clearButton);
    }
```

5. Define the constructor that will be used to instantiate the `EmployeeForm` class, as shown in the following code:

    ```
    public EmployeeForm()
    {
      createForm();
    }
    ```

6. Instantiate and add the `EmployeeForm` class in any form, panel, or a relevant widget, when necessary.

How it works...

To create any form, we can generally inherit the library class `FormPanel`, create instances for required widgets, and add the widgets in the form using some appropriate layouts—that's all what we have done in this recipe.

Let's see what we have done in the `createForm` method and how it works. Firstly, we have set some properties for the form.

The method `setFrame(boolean)` is used to render the panel. The argument is `true` to render the panel with custom-rounded borders, and `false` to render with plain 1-pixel square borders.

To set title text for a panel, the `setTitle(String)` method is used.

Labels can be placed on the left, right, or top of the field widgets. The `setLabelAlign(LabelAlign)` method does this. The appropriate parameter values are `LabelAlign.TOP`, `LabelAlign.LEFT`, and `LabelAlign.RIGHT` for aligning on the top, left, and right of the field widget, respectively

The `setButtonAlign` method sets the alignment of any buttons added to the form. This method takes `Style.HorizontalAlignment` as its parameter. Appropriate parameter values are `CENTER`, `LEFT`, and `RIGHT`.

Layouts are responsible for connecting the child components to the container. Layouts create any internal element structure by inserting its child components at appropriate locations. In this recipe, we have used `LayoutContainer`, which is a container that lays out the child components using a layout. We have set `ColumnLayout` as the layout for the `LayoutContainer`. `ColumnLayout` positions and sizes the container's child components in columns horizontally. Each child component may specify its width in pixels or as a percentage of the remaining parent width. We have divided the `FormPanel` into two columns—left and right. The width for each of the columns is set to 50 percent of the `LayoutContainer` by specifying `new ColumnData(.5)` when they are added.

In this recipe, each column is a separate layout container, and each one has its own layout, `FormLayout`. `FormLayout` is used for form fields and their labels.

The following image is a screenshot of the employee form. As we have set today's date as the maximum value, see that the dates after today's (July 23, 2010 here) are disabled.

The following screenshot shows the items of the simple combo box:

Creating a TabPanel to show forms as tabs

`TabPanel` is a basic tab container. It can contain many tab items containing other widgets. Thus, it allows the users to open more than one form at a time. In this recipe, we are going to configure the main content panel (as stated in *Chapter 2, Creating Home Page with Panels and Menus*) to `TabPanel`.

Getting ready

Open the `HomePage` class where we will do the necessary change and add the code.

How to do it...

1. Import the `TabItem` and `TabPanel` classes:

   ```
   import com.extjs.gxt.ui.client.widget.TabItem;
   import com.extjs.gxt.ui.client.widget.TabPanel;
   ```

2. Create a class-level `TabPanel` instance:

   ```
   private TabPanel tabPanel = new TabPanel();
   ```

3. Define a method `addTab` that accepts a `String` and a `ContentPanel` object as its two arguments, as in the following code:

   ```
   private void addTab(String text, ContentPanel contentPanel)
   {
     TabItem item = new TabItem();
     item.setText(text);
     item.setClosable(true);
     item.add(contentPanel);
     tabPanel.add(item);
     tabPanel.setSelection(item);
   }
   ```

4. Set the required properties for `tabpanel` in the constructor of the `HomePage` class:

   ```
   tabPanel.setMinTabWidth(115);
   tabPanel.setTabScroll(true);
   tabPanel.setCloseContextMenu(true);
   ```

5. Create a `LayoutData` instance in the constructor for adding `tabpanel` in `HomePage`:

   ```
   BorderLayoutData mainContentsLayoutData =
     new BorderLayoutData(LayoutRegion.CENTER);
   mainContentsLayoutData.setMargins(new Margins(0));
   ```

6. Add `tabPanel` in `HomePage` by writing the following code in the constructor:

```
add(tabPanel, mainContentsLayoutData);
```

How it works...

The `addTab` method will be called when a widget is required to be added as tab. The first argument, `text`, is used to pass the title text of the tab item. Tab items can be closable. The `setClosable(Boolean)` method is invoked with the parameter `true` to make a tab closable. When it is made closable by calling this method, a small "close" icon appears on the top-right corner of the tab. Widgets are added in the tab item by calling the `add` method and finally, the tab item is added in the tab panel by calling the `add` method of the `TabPanel` class. The `setSelection(TabItem)` method of the `TabPanel` class sets a tab as "selected". We have called this method in the `addTab` method to make the newly added tab as "selected".

The method `setTabScroll` with the argument `true` enables scrolling to tabs that may be invisible due to overflowing of the overall `TabPanel` width. The `setCloseContextMenu` method of the `TabPanel` class with the argument `true` adds a context menu with two options—**Close this tab** and **Close all other tabs** that are used to close a particular tab or all other tabs, respectively.

See also

▶ The *Creating a navigation sidebar with Accordion layout* recipe

Creating a navigation sidebar with Accordion layout

In our home page layout we have the provision for a sidebar. In this recipe, we are going to create sidebar for navigation.

Getting ready

Open the `HomePage` class to modify the `getLeftSidebar` method.

How to do it...

Write the following code in the `getLeftSidebar` method:

1. Create an instance of the `ContentPanel` class:

```
ContentPanel leftSidebarPanel = new ContentPanel();
```

2. Set the required properties for the left sidebar content panel, as in the following code:

```
leftSidebarPanel.setHeading("Navigation");
leftSidebarPanel.setBodyBorder(true);
```

3. Set the layout for the left sidebar content panel as shown:

```
leftSidebarPanel.setLayout(new AccordionLayout());
```

4. Create another content panel named `setupContentPanel`, and set the heading and layout for this content panel:

```
ContentPanel setupContentPanel=new ContentPanel();
setupContentPanel.setHeading("Setup");
setupContentPanel.setLayout(new RowLayout());
```

5. Create a `Button` object with event-handling code, as shown in the following code:

```
Button branchButton=new Button("Branch",
  new SelectionListener<ButtonEvent>() {
  @Override
  public void componentSelected(ButtonEvent ce)
  {
    BranchForm branchForm = new BranchForm();
    addTab("Branch",branchForm);
  }
});
```

In the same way, create a button object, which will be used as a menu item.

6. Add the button to `setupContentPanel`:

```
setupContentPanel.add(branchButton,new RowData(1,-1,
  new Margins(5,5,5,5)));
```

In the same way, add all the other buttons.

7. Add the `setupContentPanel` in `leftSideBarPanel`:

```
leftSidebarPanel.add(setupContentPanel);
```

8. Follow steps 4, 5, 6, and 7 for creating more content panels with buttons.

9. At last, return `leftSidebarPanel`:

```
return leftSidebarPanel;
```

How it works...

The preceding code creates a sidebar for navigation and when a button is clicked, a tab is opened, as shown in the following screenshot:

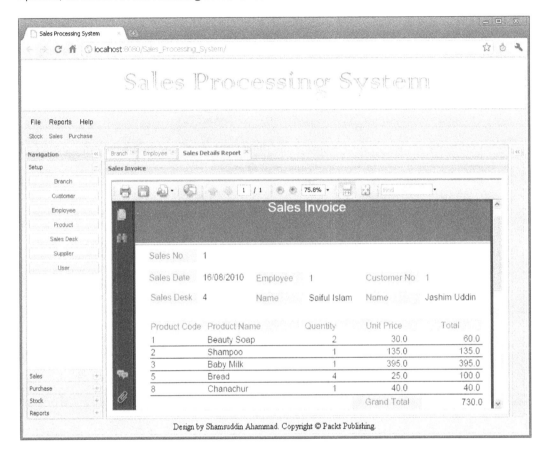

Now, let's see how these steps allow us to complete the task. Any panel with `AccordionLayout` can contain multiple content panels in an expandable accordion style such that only one panel can be open (expanded) with the other content panels collapsed, at any given point of time. The statement `leftSidebarPanel.setLayout(new AccordionLayout())` sets the layout for the left sidebar.

Each content panel (to be added in the sidebar) can have its own required layout. We have used `RowLayout` that positions the container's children in a single horizontal or vertical row. Height and width may be specified for each component in pixels or as a percentage. Each component's margin may also be specified using a `RowData` instance.

The height and width of each component can be specified with a `RowData` instance. There are three types of values:

- Values less than or equal to one are treated as percentages, with value one equivalent to 100 percent
- Values greater than one are treated as pixels
- Value -1 uses the component's computed height

We can set four side margins (left, right, top, bottom) with `RowData` for each component (button in our case here). Consider the following code:

```
setupContentPanel.add(branchButton,new RowData(1,-1,
    new Margins(5,5,5,5)));
```

It adds the branch button of 100 percent width, computed height, and a four-side margin of five pixels each. Thus, content panels are created and then added in the sidebar.

In the button event, we have called `addTab` methods for passing the instance of `BranchForm` that adds the form in the `TabPanel`. In the same way, other forms, reports, or widgets are added as a tab.

See also

- The *Creating a TabPanel to show forms as tabs* recipe

4
Handling your First Events

In this chapter, we will cover:

- ▶ Handling `ButtonEvent`
- ▶ Using the `SelectionChange` event
- ▶ Handling `FieldEvent`
- ▶ Working with the `KeyUp` event
- ▶ Handling `ChangeEvent`
- ▶ Working with `MenuEvent`
- ▶ Using `FocusEvent`
- ▶ Handling the `DatePicker` event

Introduction

The activities of a user on a User Interface (UI) are called events. Typical events include clicking on buttons, typing in text fields, selecting an item in a combo box, selecting radios, closing windows, and so on. In this chapter, we are going to handle such events in GWT.

Handling ButtonEvent

We have a button labeled as **Clear** in the **Employee** form. Now, we want the form to be reset, that is, the entire field contents should either be blank, or be filled with the default value. The default values will be set for the combo box and radio buttons when this button is clicked.

How to do it...

The code for this task can be defined within the constructor of the `SalesForm` class. The code is simply as follows:

```
clearButton.addListener(Events.Select,new Listener<ButtonEvent>()
{
  @Override
  public void handleEvent(ButtonEvent be)
  {
    employeeIdField.setValue(null);
    nameField.setValue(null);
    mobileField.setValue(null);
    emailField.setValue(null);
    dateOfBirthField.setValue(null);
    joinDateField.setValue(null);
    maleRadio.setValue(true);
    fullTimeRadio.setValue(true);
    departmentCombo.setSimpleValue("Sales");
    designationCombo.setSimpleValue("Manager");
    addressField.setValue(null);
  }
});
```

How it works...

Let's explain how these steps allow us to complete the task or solve the problem:

▶ `addListener`: This method registers a listener for the widget. This method is defined for the object `clearButton`. Thus, this button registers a listener. When the event is fired, the `handleEvent` method of the listener will be invoked automatically.

▶ `EventType`: The method `addListener` accepts two parameters. The first one is the type of event, which is of `EventType` class. There are many built-in types, such as `Blur`, `Change`, `Enable`, `Disable`, `Focus`, `KeyDown`, `KeyPress`, `KeyUp`, `Select`, `SelectionChange`, and so on. These event types are defined in the `com.extjs.gxt.ui.client.event.Events` class. In the previous code, `Select` is the event type that is used for the button.

▶ `Listener`: The next step is to implement the `Listener` function. `Listener` also requires a parameter. As we are handling the event for a button, the parameter for `Listener` is `ButtonEvent`. Other events include `BaseEvent`, `FieldEvent`, `KeyEvent`, `MenuEvent`, `PortalEvent`, and so on.

> ► handleEvent: The last step of handling the event is to override the abstract method of the `Listener` interface. The header of this method is `public void handleEvent(ButtonEvent be)`. The body section of this method contains the code for clearing the fields. The values for the text fields are set to `null`; and for the combo boxes and the radios, default values are set.

There's more...

The method we have followed in this recipe to add `Listener` is called the anonymous listener objects. Notice that we have created the `Listener` instance without giving any identifier for it. This approach is preferable when a particular `Listener` instance is used only once. Alternatively, if a `Listener` instance is reused, we can define the instance separately and register it in a widget, as follows:

```
Listener<ButtonEvent> buttonEventListener=new new
  Listener<ButtonEvent>()
{
  @Override
  public void handleEvent(ButtonEvent be)
  {
    //your code to handle events
  }
}
```

Here, we have created the `Listener` instance, which should now be registered in a component, as follows:

```
clearButton.addListener(Events.Select, buttonEventListener);
```

If this instance works for other widgets also, we should use it in the same way.

See also

- ► The *Using the SelectionChange event* recipe
- ► The *Handling FieldEvent* recipe
- ► The *Working with the KeyUp event* recipe
- ► The *Handling ChangeEvent* recipe
- ► The *Working with MenuEvent* recipe
- ► The *Using FocusEvent* recipe
- ► The *Handling the DatePicker event* recipe

Using the SelectionChange event

In the `EmployeeForm`, we have two combo boxes—one is for the department and another is for the designation. Suppose that the designations are based on the selected department, as follows:

Department	Allowable Designations
Accounts	Manager
	Officer
	Clerk
Sales	Manager
	Officer
	Salesman

Manager and officer are common designations, but a clerk works only in the accounts department, and a salesman works only in the sales department. So, when the **Accounts** department is selected from the combo box, **Salesman** should not be available as an option, and similarly, when the **Sales** department is selected, **Clerk** should not be available as an option in the allowable designations.

How to do it...

Write the following code in the constructor:

```
departmentCombo.addListener(Events.SelectionChange,new
Listener<BaseEvent>(){
  @Override
  public void handleEvent(BaseEvent be)
  {
    String department=departmentCombo.getSimpleValue().toString();
    designationCombo.removeAll();
    designationCombo.add("Manager");
    designationCombo.add("Officer");
    if(department.equalsIgnoreCase("Accounts"))
    {
      designationCombo.add("Clerk");
    }
    else if(department.equalsIgnoreCase("Sales"))
    {
      designationCombo.add("Salesman");
    }
  }
});
```

How it works...

The logic for dynamic behavior of the designation combo box is as follows:

1. Remove all elements at first.
2. Add only the allowable options.

At first, the selected value of the department is stored in a variable, then the values of the designation combo are removed. As the **Manager** and **Officer** designations are common, they are added again. The department is then checked, and options are added accordingly. In the code, it is seen that if the department is **Accounts**, the **Clerk** designation is added. If the department is **Sales**, the **Salesman** designation is added in the designation combo box.

Here, the event type is `SelectionChange` because the event will fire only when the value is changed in the department combo box.

See also

- The *Handling ButtonEvent* recipe
- The *Handling FieldEvent* recipe
- The *Working with the KeyUp event* recipe
- The *Handling ChangeEvent* recipe
- The *Working with MenuEvent* recipe
- The *Using FocusEvent* recipe
- The *Handling the DatePicker event* recipe
- The *Creating a form with two columns* recipe in *Chapter 3, Forms with Layout and Widgets*

Handling FieldEvent

Sometimes, a value for a particular field is set based on the value(s) of another (other) field(s). For example, when the quantity and price of an item are given, the total price is automatically set by multiplying the quantity and price. In this recipe, we are going to do the same thing.

Getting ready

Create a form with three fields—`priceField`, `quantityField` and `totalPriceField`.

How to do it...

Code for this recipe is as follows:

```
priceField.addListener(Events.OnBlur,new Listener<FieldEvent>(){
  @Override
  public void handleEvent(FieldEvent be)
  {
    float price=Float.parseFloat(priceField.getValue());
    int quantity=Integer.parseInt(quantityField.getValue());
    float totalPrice=price*quantity;
    addressField.setValue(String.valueOf(totalPrice));
  }
});
quantityField.addListener(Events.OnBlur,new Listener<FieldEvent>(){
  @Override
  public void handleEvent(FieldEvent be)
  {
    float price=Float.parseFloat(priceField.getValue());
    int quantity=Integer.parseInt(quantityField.getValue());
    float totalPrice=price*quantity;
    addressField.setValue(String.valueOf(totalPrice));
  }
});
```

How it works...

Here, the same code is written for both, `priceField` and `quantityField`, and the event type is `OnBlur`. Due to this, when the focus is lost from any of these, the event will fire.

Values of `priceField` and `quantityField` are stored in two variables—`price` and `quantity`, respectively. The product of these two variables is stored in the `totalPrice` variable, which is then set as the value for `totalPriceField`.

See also

- ▶ The *Handling ButtonEvent* recipe
- ▶ The *Using the SelectionChangeevent* recipe
- ▶ The *Working with the KeyUp event* recipe
- ▶ The *Handling ChangeEvent* recipe
- ▶ The *Working with MenuEvent* recipe
- ▶ The *Using FocusEvent* recipe
- ▶ The *Handling the DatePicker event* recipe

Working with the KeyUp event

While typing in text in a text field, a `KeyUp` event fires as soon as a key of the keyboard is released ("key up"). This event allows automatic update of one or more fields based on the keystroke in one field. In this recipe, we are going to use this event for calculating and showing the VAT (15 percent of the total price) and a round figure of the total price including VAT instantly when the total price is typed in a field.

Getting ready

Create a form containing three text fields for the total price, VAT, and total price including VAT respectively. Name the fields as `totalPriceField`, `vatField`, and `totalPriceIncludingVatField`.

How to do it...

Write the code, as follows:

```
totalPriceField.addListener(Events.KeyUp,new Listener<FieldEvent>(){
  @Override
  public void handleEvent(FieldEvent be)
  {
    try
    {
      double totalPrice =
        Double.parseDouble(totalPriceField.getValue());
      double vat = totalPrice*15/100;
      long totalPriceIncludingVat = Math.round(totalPrice + vat);
      vatField.setValue(String.valueOf(vat));
      totalPriceIncludingVatField.setValue(String.valueOf
        (totalPriceIncludingVat));
    }
    catch(NumberFormatException nfe)
    {
      totalPriceIncludingVatField.setValue("Wrong Value");
    }
  }
});
```

How it works...

1. The event will fire when the user types data in `totalPriceField`; that's why the event handler is defined as `FieldEvent` for `totalPriceField`.

2. The total price entered in `totalPriceField` is stored in the `double` variable, `totalPrice`, after parsing to double.

3. 15 percent VAT is calculated and stored in the variable `vat`.

4. VAT is added with the total price, the sum is rounded, and then it is stored in the `long` variable, `totalPriceIncludingVat`. When a `double` value is rounded, the round figure is of `long` type.

5. The calculated values are set in their respective fields.

If the value is wrong (other than numbers), the `NumberFormatException` exception will be thrown. To give the correct output, this exception is caught. If the exception occurs, the `totalPriceIncludingVatField` will show the string `Wrong Value`.

There's more...

There are some other keyboard events as well:

 ▶ `KeyDown`: This event fires before the `KeyPress` event fires, when a key on the keyboard is just pressed.

 ▶ `KeyPress`: This event fires after the `KeyDown` event fires, when a key on the keyboard is pressed.

 ▶ `KeyUp`: Recall that the `KeyUp` event fires when a key on the keyboard is released.

See also

 ▶ The *Handling ButtonEvent* recipe
 ▶ The *Using the SelectionChange event* recipe
 ▶ The *Handling FieldEvent* recipe
 ▶ The *Handling ChangeEvent* recipe
 ▶ The *Working with MenuEvent* recipe
 ▶ The *Using FocusEvent* recipe
 ▶ The *Handling the DatePicker event* recipe

Handling ChangeEvent

In this recipe, we are going to handle `ChangeEvent` for a `CheckBox`. When a checkbox is checked or unchecked, the `ChangeEvent` event fires. This recipe enables and disables a text field when the check box is checked and unchecked, respectively.

Getting ready

Create a form with a `CheckBox` and a `TextField`. Name the widgets as `otherCheckBox` and `otherField`. Set the box label as `Other` for the check box.

How to do it...

Write the following code for the recipe:

```
otherCheckBox.addListener(Events.Change,new Listener<BaseEvent>()
{
  @Override
  public void handleEvent(BaseEvent be)
  {
    if(otherCheckBox.getValue())
      otherField.enable();
    else
      otherField.disable();
  }
});
```

How it works...

The method `getValue` of `CheckBox` returns Boolean `true` when the check box is checked, and false when it is unchecked. If the condition `otherCheckBox.getValue()` is true, the text field is enabled by calling the `enable` method of the text field. If the condition is false, the `else` section will work and `disable` the field.

See also

 ▸ The *Handling ButtonEvent* recipe
 ▸ The *Using the SelectionChange event* recipe
 ▸ The *Handling FieldEvent* recipe
 ▸ The *Working with the KeyUp event* recipe
 ▸ The *Working with MenuEvent* recipe

- ▸ The *Using FocusEvent* recipe
- ▸ The *Handling the DatePickerevent* recipe

Working with MenuEvent

In this recipe, we are going to learn how to handle the `MenuEvent` event. We will show the `EmployeeForm` in the main content panel area of our `HomePage` when the `Employee` menu item is clicked.

Getting ready

Create a `MenuItem` labeled `Employee`, add the menu item in the `File` menu, and create the `EmployeeForm`.

How to do it...

Write the following code where appropriate:

```
employeeMenuItem.addListener(Events.Select,new Listener<MenuEvent>()
{
  @Override
  public void handleEvent(MenuEvent me)
  {
    EmployeeForm employeeForm=new EmployeeForm();
    addTab("Employee",employeeForm);
  }
});
```

How it works...

The `handleEvent` method of `Listener` of type `MenuEvent` is overridden here. When the event fires, an instance of `EmployeeForm` class is created and is added on the tab panel at the center of the home page (instance of `com.extjs.gxt.ui.client.widget.TabPanel`) as a tab item.

See also

- ▸ The *Handling ButtonEvent* recipe
- ▸ The *Using the SelectionChange event* recipe

- ► The *Handling FieldEvent* recipe
- ► The *Working with the KeyUp event* recipe
- ► The *Handling ChangeEvent* recipe
- ► The *Using FocusEvent* recipe
- ► The *Handling the DatePicker event* recipe
- ► The *Creating a TabPanel to show forms as tabs* recipe in chapter 3
- ► The *Creating a navigation sidebar with Accordion layout* recipe in chapter 3

Using FocusEvent

FocusEvent fires when a component (for example TextField) gains focus, that is, the cursor moves to the component. Suppose we have two fields—one each for the product ID and product price. When the product price receives focus after giving the product ID, the price of the product will be automatically shown. In most cases, the product price will come from the database or the file, but in this example, it is static and hard coded.

How to do it...

Write the following code for the recipe:

```
priceField.addListener(Events.Focus,new Listener<FieldEvent>()
{
  @Override
  public void handleEvent(FieldEvent fe)
  {
    int productId=Integer.parseInt(productIdField.getValue());
    if(productId==1)
      priceField.setValue(String.valueOf(500));
    else if(productId==2)
      priceField.setValue(String.valueOf(800));
    else if(productId==3)
      priceField.setValue(String.valueOf(1500));
  }
});
```

How it works...

Here, a listener has been registered in the `price` field. Notice that the event type is `Focus`. In the `handleEvent` method, the following is done:

- ▸ Store the user input in the `productId` variable after converting the `String` value to `int`.

- ▸ The value of the `productId` variable is compared with the static values 1, 2, or 3. A value is set in the `price` field based on the value of the product ID.

See also

- ▸ The *Handling ButtonEvent* recipe
- ▸ The *Using the SelectionChange event* recipe
- ▸ The *Handling FieldEvent* recipe
- ▸ The *Working with the KeyUp event* recipe
- ▸ The *Handling ChangeEvent* recipe
- ▸ The *Working with Menu Event* recipe
- ▸ The *Handling the DatePickerEvent* recipe

Handling the DatePicker event

In this recipe, we are going to calculate the age of a person when the date of birth is given in `DateField`.

Getting ready

For this example, it is assumed that:

- ▸ `dateOfBirtField` is an instance of the `com.extjs.gxt.ui.client.widget.form.DateField` class

- ▸ `ageField` is an instance of the `com.extjs.gxt.ui.client.widget.form.TextField` class

How to do it...

The code for this recipe is as follows:

```
dateOfBirthField.getDatePicker().addListener
  (Events.Select,new Listener<DatePickerEvent>()
{
```

```
@Override
public void handleEvent(DatePickerEvent be)
{
  Date today=new Date();
  Date dob=dateOfBirthField.getValue();

  long difference=today.getTime()-dob.getTime();

  long second=difference/1000;
  long minute=second/60;
  long hour=minute/60;
  long day=hour/24;

  long month=day/30;
  day=day%30;

  long year=month/12;
   month=month%12;
  ageField.setValue(year+" year "+month+" month
    "+day+" day");
 }
}) ;
```

How it works...

Let's explain how these steps allow us to complete the task or solve the problem.

- DatePicker: In the form for giving the input date of birth, we have used
  DateField, which is composed of several parts, and DatePicker is one of them.
  The field we type in is a TextField. As the event will fire in the DatePicker
  instance, we need to get the DatePicker object from the DateField. By
  writing dateOfBirthField.getDatePicker(), we have the reference to the
  DatePicker object of the dateOfBirthField.

- Listener: For this event, the event type is com.extjs.gxt.ui.client.event.
  Events.Select, and the parameter for the Listener is DatePickerEvent.
  The code dateOfBirthField.getDatePicker().addListener(Events.
  Select,new Listener<DatePickerEvent>() does this.

- Calculating Age: The steps for calculating the age are as follows:

  - Get the current date, for which the code is as follows:

    ```
    Date today=new Date();
    ```
  - Get the input date of birth, for which the code is as follows:

    ```
    Date dob=dateOfBirthField.getValue();
    ```
  - Get the time for each date and the difference by deducting the time of the
    date of birth from the time of today. The following code does this task:

    ```
    long difference=today.getTime()-dob.getTime()
    ```

Here, we get the time and the difference in milliseconds.

❑ The next step is to convert the milliseconds to year, month, and day. In this example, for converting the leap year, 28 or 31 number of days per month are ignored as they are calculated from milliseconds.

❑ Showing the age in the text field using the code:

```
ageField.setValue(year+"" year ""+month+"" month ""+day+"
day"")
```

See also

▶ The *Handling ButtonEvent* recipe

▶ The *Using the SelectionChangeEvent* recipe

▶ The *Handling FieldEvent* recipe

▶ The *Working with the KeyUp Event* recipe

▶ The *Handling ChangeEvent* recipe

▶ The *Working with MenuEvent* recipe

▶ The *Using FocusEvent* recipe

5
Creating Database for Sales Processing

In this chapter, we will cover:

- ▸ Creating a database
- ▸ Creating tables with primary keys
- ▸ Defining foreign keys
- ▸ Backing up the database
- ▸ Restoring the database

Introduction

A database is the key part of a business application. A well-designed database maintains the business data in a proper way, so that it can be used further for any business information efficiently. The database part of the business application is called the **backend** and the user interface part is the **frontend**.

In this chapter, we will design a database for a sales processing system and create a database in the MySQL server that we installed in *Chapter 1, Setting up GWT Environment in NetBeans*.

Designing the database for sales processing

Designing the database includes identifying the business entities, the relationships among the entities, constraints of the entities, and so on.

An entity resides in a table. In our sales processing system, we are going to create the following tables based on the identified business entities:

- **Branch**: This table will hold the branch ID, name, and location of each branch of an organization. Sales of each branch will be tracked.

- **Employee**: This table will hold information of all employees, such as managers, salesmen, and so on.

- **Supplier**: This table will hold details of suppliers from whom the products are purchased.

- **Customer**: This table will hold the customer details.

- **Product**: This table will hold product information, such as product ID, name, and category.

- **Stock**: This table will hold stock information for each product.

- **Sales desk**: This table will hold information about the point where sales are made.

- **Sales**: This table will hold information particular to each sale, such as sales ID, concerned salesman, and sales.

- **Sales details**: This table will hold information of sold products, such as quantity and price.

- **Purchase**: This table will hold the purchase number, purchase date, and so on, of products when they are added to stock.

- **Purchase details**: This table will hold information of purchased products, their quantity, and the price.

- **Users**: This table will store the login credentials of the users of the system.

Entity Relationships Diagram (**ERD**) is a suitable tool to represent the database structure including, the tables, attributes, primary keys, foreign keys, and so on. Following is the ERD for our system.

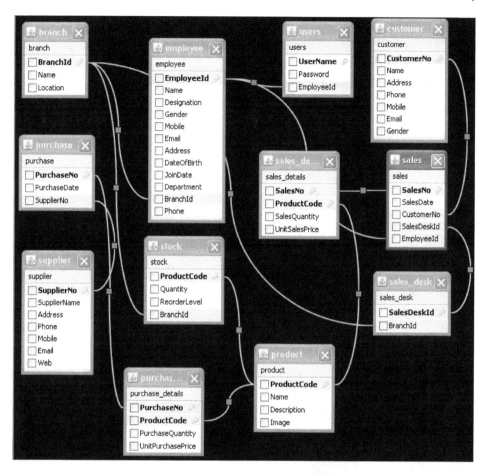

Creating the database

In this recipe, we are going to create a database called **Sales**.

Getting ready

Make sure that MySQL GUI Tools are installed.

How to do it...

1. Start **MySQL Query Browser**.

2. Right-click on **Schemata** and select **Create New Schema**.

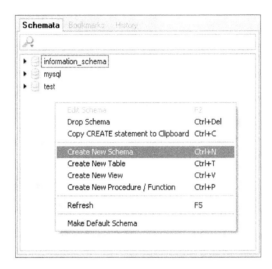

3. In the input dialog, enter **Sales** as the **Schema name**.

4. Click on **OK**. A new database, **Sales**, is created.

There's more...

It is possible to create the database from command tools, that is, without using the GUI environment. Knowledge of SQL is necessary to use the command tools. When we use the GUI tools, the required SQL command is generated automatically; but in command tools, every SQL command is written by us.

Creating database using MySQL Command Line Client

1. Start the MySQL Command Line Client from **Start** | **All Programs** | **MySQL** | **MySQL Server 5.1**.

2. Enter the root password

3. Execute the following command:

   `CREATE DATABASE Sales;`

 Don't forget to add a semicolon (;) after the command here. This is needed by the MySQL client to understand where the end of the command is.

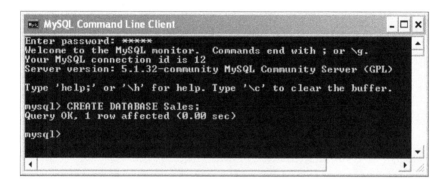

▸ The *Creating tables with primary key* recipe

▸ The *Defining foreign keys* recipe

Creating tables with primary key

In this recipe, we are going to create the table, **Branch**.

How to do it...

1. Start the **MySQL Query Browser**.

2. Double-click on **Sales** in **Schemata** to select the database.

3. Right-click on the **Sales** database and select **Create New Table**.

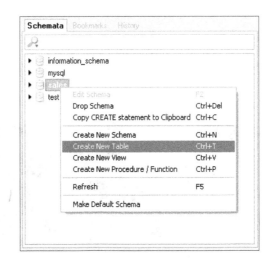

4. In the **Table Editor**, specify the **Column Name**, **Datatype**, and other constraints, as shown in the following screenshot:

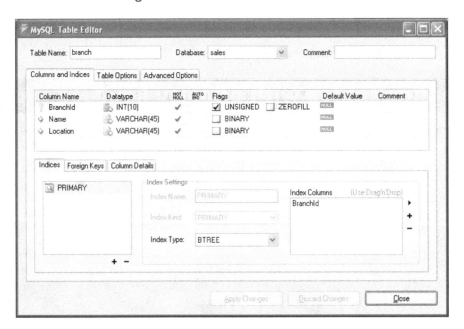

5. A "key" symbol is present on the left-hand side of the **BranchId** column name. This is the symbol for **Primary Key**. To set a primary key, just click on the icon appearing on the left-hand side of the column name.

6. Click on **Apply Changes** to create the table.

7. Click on **Close**.

Creating tables from MySQL Command Line Client

To create the Branch table from the Command Line Client, carry out the following steps:

1. Start MySQL Command Line Client.

2. Enter the Password.

3. Change the database to **Sales** by writing the following command:

   ```
   USE Sales;
   ```

4. Execute the following command:

   ```
   CREATE TABLE  `sales`.`branch` (
     `BranchId` int(10) unsigned NOT NULL,
     `Name` varchar(45) NOT NULL,
     `Location` varchar(45) NOT NULL,
     PRIMARY KEY (`BranchId`)
   ) ENGINE=InnoDB DEFAULT CHARSET=latin1;
   ```

See also

▸ The *Defining foreign keys* recipe

Defining foreign keys

In this recipe, we are going to create the Employee table with the foreign key attribute, namely, `BranchId`.

Getting ready

Open the **MySQL Query Browser** and create the employee table, as we did in the preceding recipe.

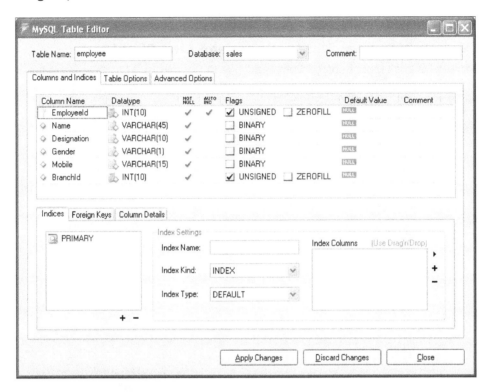

How to do it...

1. Select the **Foreign Keys** tab.
2. Press the **+** (plus) symbol at the bottom.
3. Enter **FK_Employee_Branch_BranchId** as the **Foreign Key Name**.

4. Click on **OK**.

5. Select **Branch** from the **Ref. Table**.

6. Select **Restrict** from the **On Delete** combo box.

7. Select **Cascade** from the **On Update** combo box.

8. Click on **Apply Changes | Execute**.

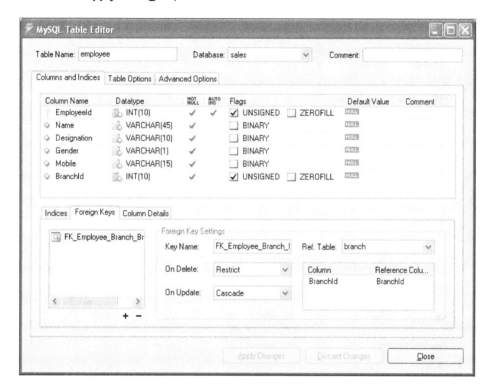

9. Click on **Close**.

There's more...

In this same way, all the other tables have to be created.

Creating all the other tables using MySQL Query Browser

Create all the tables as shown in the following screenshots in this section. Alternatively, you can download the SQL script from the Packt website to create all the tables instantly. To use the script, follow the *Restoring the database* recipe.

Table Name: stock

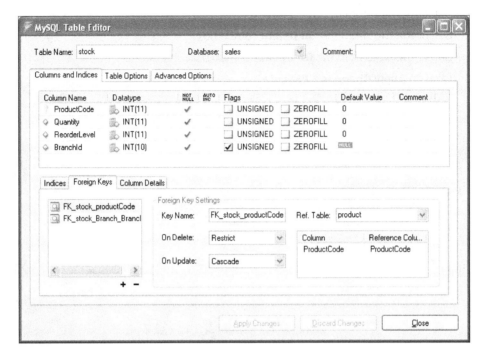

Table Name: supplier

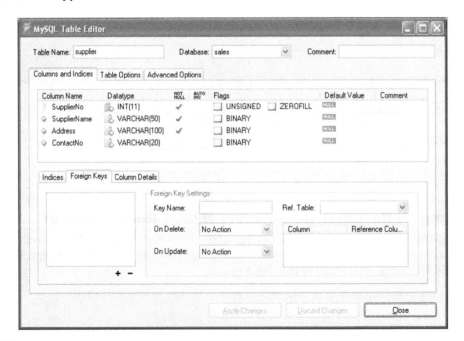

Table Name: customer

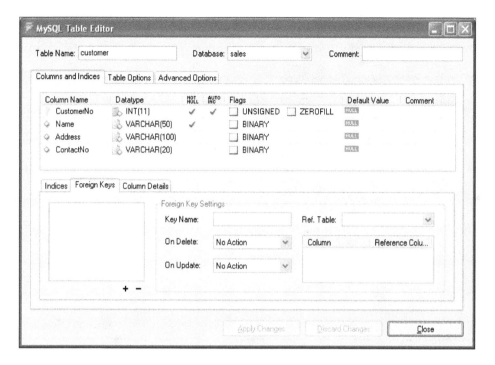

Table Name: sales_desk

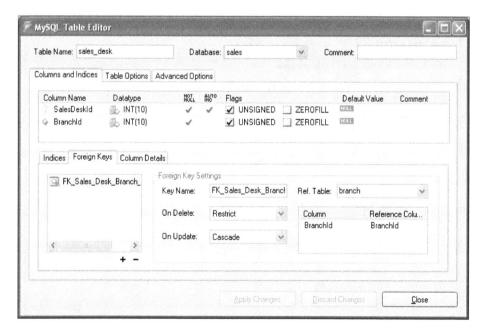

Table Name: purchase

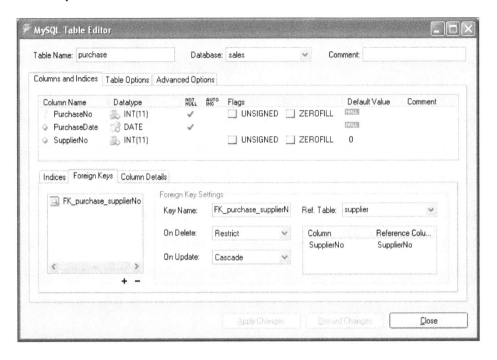

Table Name: purchase_details

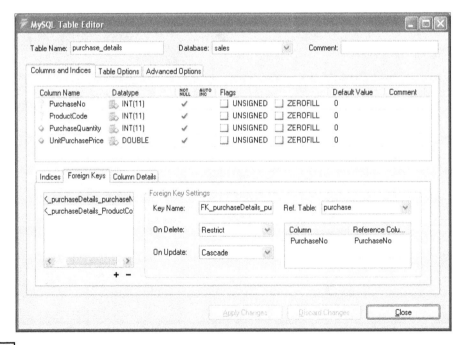

Table Name: sales

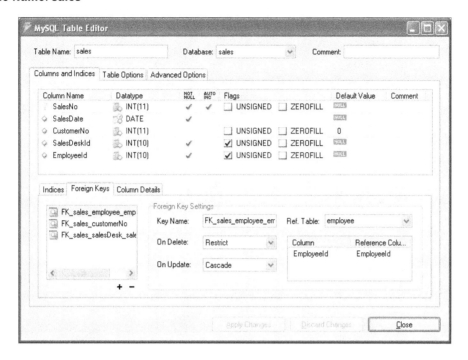

Table Name: sales_details

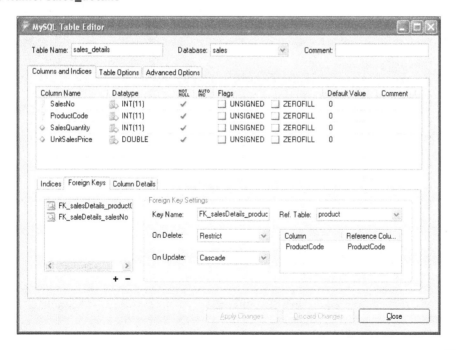

Table Name: users

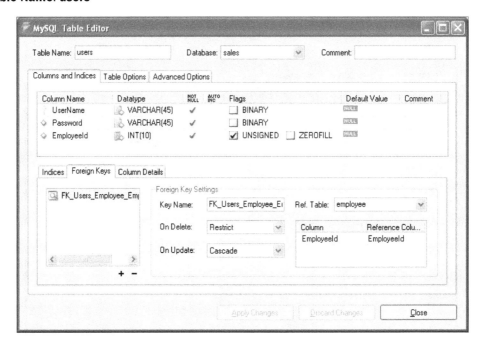

Creating all the other tables in Command Client

To create all the other tables, execute the following commands. You can also download the script from the Packt website. The script will help you to create the tables quickly. To use the script, follow the *Restoring the database* recipe.

```
CREATE TABLE `customer` (
  `CustomerNo` int(11) NOT NULL AUTO_INCREMENT,
  `Name` varchar(50) NOT NULL,
  `Address` varchar(100) DEFAULT NULL,
  `ContactNo` varchar(20) DEFAULT NULL,
  PRIMARY KEY (`CustomerNo`)
) ENGINE=InnoDB DEFAULT CHARSET=utf8 ROW_FORMAT=FIXED;

CREATE TABLE `employee` (
  `EmployeeId` int(10) unsigned NOT NULL AUTO_INCREMENT,
  `Name` varchar(45) NOT NULL,
  `Designation` varchar(10) NOT NULL,
  `Gender` varchar(1) NOT NULL,
  `Mobile` varchar(15) NOT NULL,
  `BranchId` int(10) unsigned NOT NULL,
  PRIMARY KEY (`EmployeeId`),
  KEY `FK_Employee_Branch_BranchId` (`BranchId`),
  CONSTRAINT `FK_Employee_Branch_BranchId` FOREIGN KEY (`BranchId`)
REFERENCES `branch` (`BranchId`) ON UPDATE CASCADE
) ENGINE=InnoDB DEFAULT CHARSET=latin1;
```

```
CREATE TABLE `product` (
  `ProductCode` int(11) NOT NULL,
  `Name` varchar(50) NOT NULL,
  `Description` varchar(50) DEFAULT NULL,
  `Image` longblob,
  PRIMARY KEY (`ProductCode`) USING BTREE
  ) ENGINE=InnoDB DEFAULT CHARSET=utf8;

CREATE TABLE `purchase` (
  `PurchaseNo` int(11) NOT NULL,
  `PurchaseDate` date NOT NULL,
  `SupplierNo` int(11) DEFAULT '0',
  PRIMARY KEY (`PurchaseNo`) USING BTREE,
  KEY `supplierNo` (`SupplierNo`) USING BTREE,
  KEY `FK_purchase_supplierNo` (`SupplierNo`),
  CONSTRAINT `FK_purchase_supplierNo` FOREIGN KEY (`SupplierNo`)
  REFERENCES `supplier` (`SupplierNo`) ON UPDATE CASCADE
  ) ENGINE=InnoDB DEFAULT CHARSET=utf8 ROW_FORMAT=FIXED;

CREATE TABLE `purchase_details` (
  `PurchaseNo` int(11) NOT NULL DEFAULT '0',
  `ProductCode` int(11) NOT NULL DEFAULT '0',
  `PurchaseQuantity` int(11) NOT NULL DEFAULT '0',
  `UnitPurchasePrice` double NOT NULL DEFAULT '0',
  PRIMARY KEY (`PurchaseNo`,`ProductCode`) USING BTREE,
  KEY `purchaseNo` (`PurchaseNo`) USING BTREE,
  KEY `productNo` (`ProductCode`) USING BTREE,
  KEY `FK_purchaseline_purchaseNo` (`PurchaseNo`),
  CONSTRAINT `FK_purchaseDetails_purchaseNo`
  FOREIGN KEY (`PurchaseNo`) REFERENCES `purchase` (`PurchaseNo`)
  ON UPDATE CASCADE,
  CONSTRAINT `FK_purchaseDetails_ProductCode`
  FOREIGN KEY (`ProductCode`) REFERENCES `product` (`ProductCode`)
  ON UPDATE CASCADE
  ) ENGINE=InnoDB DEFAULT CHARSET=utf8 ROW_FORMAT=FIXED;

CREATE TABLE `sales` (
  `SalesNo` int(11) NOT NULL AUTO_INCREMENT,
  `SalesDate` date NOT NULL,
  `CustomerNo` int(11) DEFAULT '0',
  `SalesDeskId` int(10) unsigned NOT NULL,
  `EmployeeId` int(10) unsigned NOT NULL,
  PRIMARY KEY (`SalesNo`) USING BTREE,
  KEY `customerNo` (`CustomerNo`) USING BTREE,
  KEY `FK_sales_customerNo` (`CustomerNo`),
  KEY `FK_sales_salesDesk_salesDeskId` (`SalesDeskId`),
  KEY `FK_sales_employee_employeeId` (`EmployeeId`),

  CONSTRAINT `FK_sales_employee_employeeId`
```

```
  FOREIGN KEY (`EmployeeId`) REFERENCES `employee` (`EmployeeId`)
  ON UPDATE CASCADE,
  CONSTRAINT `FK_sales_customerNo` FOREIGN KEY (`CustomerNo`)
  REFERENCES `customer` (`CustomerNo`) ON UPDATE CASCADE,

  CONSTRAINT `FK_sales_salesDesk_salesDeskId`
  FOREIGN KEY (`SalesDeskId`) REFERENCES `sales_desk` (`SalesDeskId`)
  ON UPDATE CASCADE
  ) ENGINE=InnoDB DEFAULT CHARSET=utf8 ROW_FORMAT=FIXED;

CREATE TABLE `sales_desk` (
  `SalesDeskId` int(10) unsigned NOT NULL AUTO_INCREMENT,
  `BranchId` int(10) unsigned NOT NULL,
  PRIMARY KEY (`SalesDeskId`),
  KEY `FK_Sales_Desk_Branch_BranchId` (`BranchId`),
  CONSTRAINT `FK_Sales_Desk_Branch_BranchId`
  FOREIGN KEY (`BranchId`) REFERENCES `branch` (`BranchId`)
  ON UPDATE CASCADE
  ) ENGINE=InnoDB DEFAULT CHARSET=latin1;

CREATE TABLE `sales_details` (
  `SalesNo` int(11) NOT NULL DEFAULT '0',
  `ProductCode` int(11) NOT NULL DEFAULT '0',
  `SalesQuantity` int(11) NOT NULL DEFAULT '0',
  `UnitSalesPrice` double NOT NULL DEFAULT '0',
  PRIMARY KEY (`SalesNo`,`ProductCode`) USING BTREE,
  KEY `salesNo` (`SalesNo`) USING BTREE,
  KEY `productNo` (`ProductCode`) USING BTREE,
  KEY `FK_salesline_productCode` (`ProductCode`),
  KEY `FK_salesline_salesNo` (`SalesNo`),
  CONSTRAINT `FK_salesDetails_productCode`
  FOREIGN KEY (`ProductCode`) REFERENCES `product` (`ProductCode`)
  ON UPDATE CASCADE,
  CONSTRAINT `FK_saleDetails_salesNo`
  FOREIGN KEY (`SalesNo`) REFERENCES `sales` (`SalesNo`)
  ON UPDATE CASCADE
  ) ENGINE=InnoDB DEFAULT CHARSET=utf8 ROW_FORMAT=FIXED;

CREATE TABLE `stock` (
  `ProductCode` int(11) NOT NULL DEFAULT '0',
  `Quantity` int(11) NOT NULL DEFAULT '0',
  `ReorderLevel` int(11) NOT NULL DEFAULT '0',
  `BranchId` int(10) unsigned NOT NULL,
  PRIMARY KEY (`ProductCode`) USING BTREE,
  UNIQUE KEY `productNo` (`ProductCode`) USING BTREE,
  KEY `FK_stock_productCode` (`ProductCode`),
  KEY `FK_stock_Branch_BranchId` (`BranchId`),
  CONSTRAINT `FK_stock_Branch_BranchId` FOREIGN KEY (`BranchId`)
  REFERENCES `branch` (`BranchId`) ON UPDATE CASCADE,
```

```
  CONSTRAINT `FK_stock_productCode` FOREIGN KEY (`ProductCode`)
  REFERENCES `product` (`ProductCode`) ON UPDATE CASCADE
  ) ENGINE=InnoDB DEFAULT CHARSET=utf8 ROW_FORMAT=FIXED;

CREATE TABLE `supplier` (
  `SupplierNo` int(11) NOT NULL,
  `SupplierName` varchar(50) NOT NULL,
  `Address` varchar(100) NOT NULL,
  `ContactNo` varchar(20) DEFAULT NULL,
  PRIMARY KEY (`SupplierNo`)
  ) ENGINE=InnoDB DEFAULT CHARSET=utf8 ROW_FORMAT=FIXED;

CREATE TABLE `users` (
  `UserName` varchar(45) NOT NULL,
  `Password` varchar(45) NOT NULL,
  `EmployeeId` int(10) unsigned NOT NULL,
  PRIMARY KEY (`UserName`),
  KEY `FK_Users_Employee_EmployeeId` (`EmployeeId`),
  CONSTRAINT `FK_Users_Employee_EmployeeId`
  FOREIGN KEY (`EmployeeId`) REFERENCES `employee` (`EmployeeId`)
  ON UPDATE CASCADE
  ) ENGINE=InnoDB DEFAULT CHARSET=latin1;
```

Backing up database

Most often, we may need to transfer the database from one PC to another PC. Backup and restore tools help to transfer the database (with or without data). Basically, the backup tools create a file containing the SQL command for creating database, creating tables, and populating the database with data. The restore tools read the file and create the same, according to the commands given in the file.

In this recipe, we are going to Backup the database we have created in the earlier recipes. In the following recipe, we will restore this database.

How to do it...

1. Start **MySQL Administrator**.
2. Go to **Backup**.
3. Click on **New Project**.
4. Give **Sales** as **Project Name**.
5. Select **Sales** database from **Schemata** and press the **>** (right arrow) button.
6. Click on **Save Project**.

7. Click on **Execute Backup Now**.

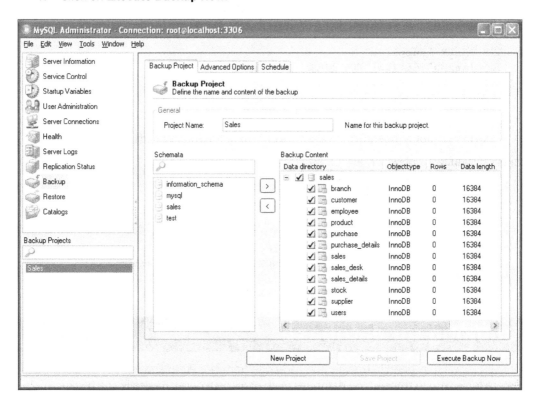

8. Select the required directory and click on **Save**.

How it works...

A text file with SQL commands to create the full database has been created. This file will now be used to restore the database.

See also

▸ The *Restoring the database* recipe

Restoring database

In this recipe, we are going to restore database using the file created in the previous recipe.

Getting ready

For the experiment, we will drop the existing sales database.

1. Start MySQL Query Browser.
2. Right-click on **Sales** database in **Schemata**.
3. Click on **Drop Schema**.

How to do it...

1. Start MySQL Administrator.
2. Go to **Restore**.

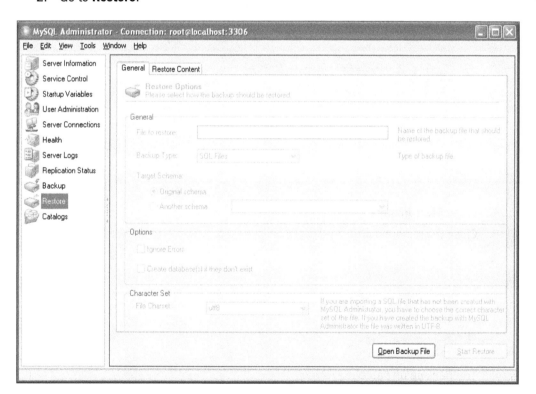

3. Press **Open Backup File** and select the file.

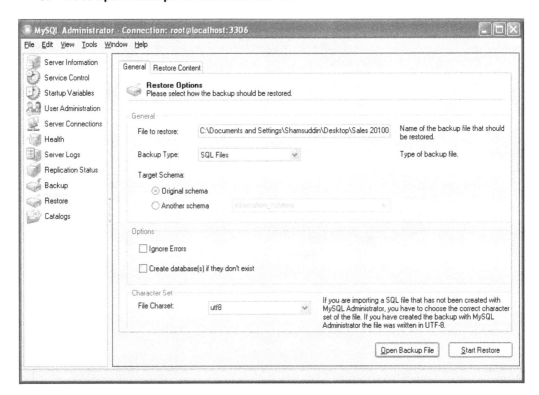

4. Press **Start Restore**.
5. Close the restore dialog.

How it works...

Each command in the file is executed to create the database and the tables.

See also

▶ The *Backing up database* recipe

6

Managing Entities
using JPA

In this chapter, we will cover:

- ▶ Creating a database connection in NetBeans
- ▶ Creating a persistence unit
- ▶ Creating entity classes from the database
- ▶ Creating controller classes

Introduction

Java Persistence API (JPA) is a framework that is used to manage relational data in Java EE and Java SE applications. JPA provides a Plain Old Java Object (POJO) persistence model for object relational mapping.

JPA in GWT

In the perspective of the GWT, JPA will provide data operations on the server based on the client request. If a relational database is used in the application, JPA will manage the relational data on the server. It enables the developer to define the database CRUD (Create, Read, Update, and Delete) functions in a purely object-oriented fashion.

Uses

In the GWT application, following are some of the uses of JPA:

- To create entity classes
- To create the `EntityManagerFactory`
- To create the `EntityManager`
- To persist, find, merge, and remove entities
- To execute native SQL

Creating a database connection in NetBeans

A NetBeans database connection can be re-used in many other applications created in NetBeans. The database can also be explored from NetBeans when a connection is created. In this chapter, we will use the connection to generate the JPA entity classes from the database automatically.

Getting ready

Before following the recipe, the database should be created completely with all the required tables, attributes, and constraints.

How to do it...

The steps required to complete the task are listed as follows:

1. Go to **Window | Services**.
2. Right-click on **Databases** on the **Services** tab placed on the top left side of the screen and select **New Connection...**, as shown in the following screenshot:

3. In the **New Database Connection** dialog, set the following values, as shown in the screenshot following the table:

Item	Value
Data Input Mode	**Field Entry**
Driver Name	**MySQL (Connector/J Driver)**
Host	**localhost**
Port	**3306**
Database	**Sales**
Username	**root**
Password	**• • • • •**
Remember Password	**Checked on**

4. Click on **OK**. The connection is now listed under **Databases**, as shown in the following screenshot:

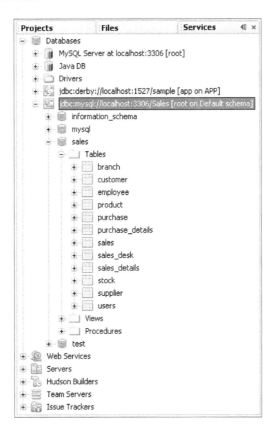

Direct URL Entry

Java programmers are habituated to write the direct JDBC URL in database applications. It's also possible to create a database connection in NetBeans. In that case, the following values should be set, as we see in the following screenshot:

Item	Value
Data Input Mode	Direct URL Entry
Driver Name	MySQL (Connector/J Driver)
Username	root
Password	• • • • •
Remember Password	Checked on
JDBC URL	jdbc:mysql://localhost:3306/Sales

Creating a persistence unit

A persistence unit is a collection of properties that are used to manage and persist the entities. Persistence units are defined in the `persistence.xml` file, where each persistence unit must have a unique name.

The properties included in the persistence unit include the following:

- A list of the entity classes
- The library or the persistence provider
- The data source used for persistent storage of the managed entities
- The transaction type

Getting ready

Before following this recipe, the database connection `jdbc:mysql://localhost:3306/Sales` should be created.

How to do it...

1. Go to **File | New File...**.
2. Select **Sales Processing System** from the **Project** drop-down list.

3. Select **Persistence** from the **Categories** list.

4. Select **Persistence Unit** from the **File Types** list, as shown in the following screenshot:

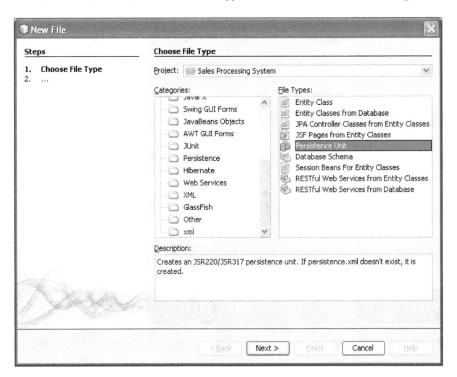

5. Click on **Next**.

6. Leave the **Persistence Unit Name** as suggested.

7. Select **EclipseLink** from the **Persistence Provider** drop-down list.

8. Select **New Data Source** from the **Data Source** drop-down list.

9. In the **Create Data Source** dialog, give **sales** as the **JNDI Name**.

10. Select **jdbc:mysql://localhost:3306/Sales** from the **Database Connection** field, as shown in the following screenshot:

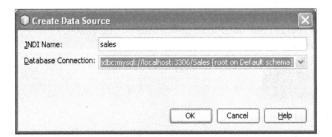

11. Click on **OK**.
12. Check on **Use Java Transaction APIs**.
13. Select **None** from **Table Generation Strategy**.

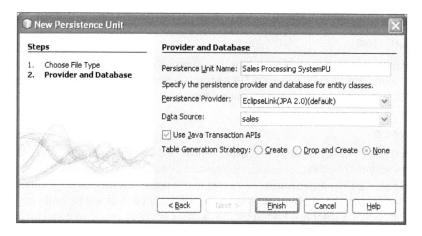

14. Click on **Finish**.

How it works...

For creating the persistence unit, the **persistence.xml** and **sun-resources.xml** files are created in the project under **Configuration Files** and **Server Resources** respectively, as shown in the following screenshot:

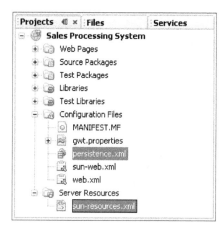

These two files are used further for managing entity classes and deploying the project on the server.

EclipseLink

The Eclipse Persistence Services Project named EclipseLink at the Eclipse Foundation provides Java persistence solution services. The services include Object Relational, Object-XML Binding, Service Data Objects, and Web Services for RDBMS. The Object Relational service is called the EclipseLink JPA. EclipseLink is based on the Oracle's product, TopLink.

EclipseLink JPA

The EclipseLink JPA provides support to the developers to manage the relational data in Java applications using the Java Persistence API as the reference implementation. EclipseLink JPA enables the creation of the persistence unit on the server side of the GWT application.

Data source

Official Java documentation states that "Data Source is a factory for connections to the physical data source that this `DataSource` object represents. An alternative to the `DriverManager` facility, a `DataSource` object is the preferred means of getting a connection. An object that implements the `DataSource` interface will typically be registered with a naming service based on the JavaTM Naming and Directory (JNDI) API."

persistence.xml

Contents of the file `persistence.xml` are as follows:

```xml
<?xml version="1.0" encoding="UTF-8"?>
<persistence version="2.0"
  xmlns="http://java.sun.com/xml/ns/persistence"
  xmlns:xsi="http://www.w3.org/2001/XMLSchema-instance"
  xsi:schemaLocation="http://java.sun.com/xml/ns/persistence
  http://java.sun.com/xml/ns/persistence/persistence_2_0.xsd">
    <persistence-unit name="Sales Processing SystemPU"
      transaction-type="JTA">
    <provider>org.eclipse.persistence.jpa.PersistenceProvider
    </provider>
    <jta-data-source>sales</jta-data-source>
    <exclude-unlisted-classes>false</exclude-unlisted-classes>
  </persistence-unit>
</persistence>
```

In this generated code, the persistence unit name is defined as `Sales Processing SystemPU`, which will be used for creating the entity manager factory. Java Transaction API (`JTA`) is used as the type of transaction. The line `<exclude-unlisted-classes> false` means that all of the entity class in the context will be included automatically. We will not need to add the entity classes one-by-one.

sun-resources.xml

The file `sun-resources.xml` is used to configure the server of the application. Properties for the database connection, JNDI, and so on are set in this file. When the application is deployed automatically by the IDE, the server is configured first based on this file. If we deploy the application manually, we must configure the server manually. *Chapter 9, Deploying a GWT Application* describes how to configure the server for deployment.

Contents of this file are as follows:

```xml
<?xml version="1.0" encoding="UTF-8"?>
<!DOCTYPE resources PUBLIC "-//Sun Microsystems, Inc.//DTD
  Application Server 9.0 Resource Definitions //EN"
  "http://www.sun.com/software/appserver/dtds/sun-resources_1_3.dtd">
<resources>
  <jdbc-connection-pool allow-non-component-callers="false"
    associate-with-thread="false"
    connection-creation-retry-attempts="0"
    connection-creation-retry-interval-in-seconds="10"
    connection-leak-reclaim="false"
    connection-leak-timeout-in-seconds="0"
    connection-validation-method="auto-commit"
    datasource-classname="com.mysql.jdbc.jdbc2.optional.
    MysqlDataSource" fail-all-connections="false"
    idle-timeout-in-seconds="300"
    is-connection-validation-required="false"
    is-isolation-level-guaranteed="true"
    lazy-connection-association="false"
    lazy-connection-enlistment="false"
    match-connections="false"
    max-connection-usage-count="0"
    max-pool-size="32"
    max-wait-time-in-millis="60000"
    name="mysql_Sales_rootPool"
    non-transactional-connections="false"
    pool-resize-quantity="2"
    res-type="javax.sql.DataSource"
    statement-timeout-in-seconds="-1"
    steady-pool-size="8"
    validate-atmost-once-period-in-seconds="0"
    wrap-jdbc-objects="false">
    <property name="serverName" value="localhost"/>
    <property name="portNumber" value="3306"/>
    <property name="databaseName" value="Sales"/>
    <property name="User" value="root"/>
    <property name="Password" value="shams"/>
    <property name="URL" value="jdbc:mysql://localhost:3306/Sales"/>
    <property name="driverClass" value="com.mysql.jdbc.Driver"/>
  </jdbc-connection-pool>
```

```
    <jdbc-resource enabled="true" jndi-name="sales" object-type="user"
pool-name="mysql_Sales_rootPool"/>
    </resources>
```

Creating entity classes from the database

In this recipe, we are going to create all entity classes of the `Sales` database automatically by using some easy steps in a wizard.

Getting ready

The persistence unit should be created before going to create entity classes.

How to do it...

1. Go to **File | New File...**.
2. Select **Sales Processing System** from the **Project** drop-down list.
3. Select **Persistence** from the **Categories** list.
4. Select **Entity Classes from Database** from the **File Types** list, as shown in the following screenshot:

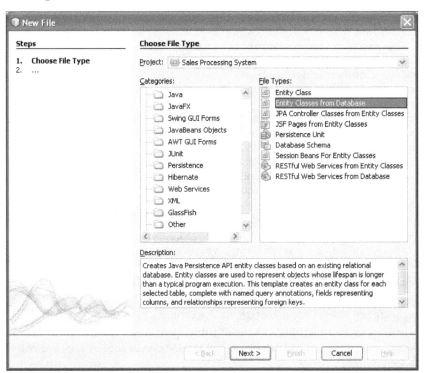

5. Click on **Next**.

6. Select **sales** from the **Data Source** field.

7. Click on the **Add All>>** button to select all the available tables:

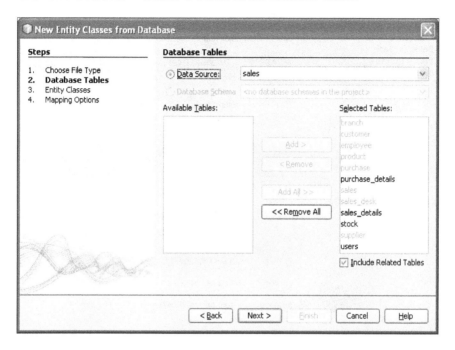

8. Click on **Next**.

9. Check the suggested class names. If they are according to the Java naming convention (which they are supposed to be), leave them as is; otherwise, modify those names.

10. Select **com.packtpub.beans** as the **Package**.

11. Check on **Generate Named Query Annotations for Persistent Fields**.

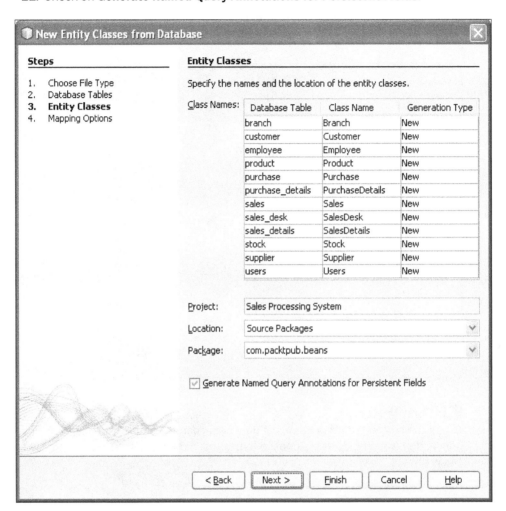

12. Click on **Next**.

13. Select **default** from **Association Fetch**.

14. Select **java.util.List** from **Collection Type**, as seen in the following screenshot:

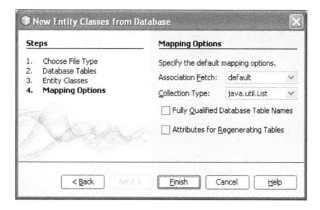

15. Click on **Finish**.

How it works...

The preceding steps create the entity classes in the **com.packtpub.beans** package, shown in the following screenshot:

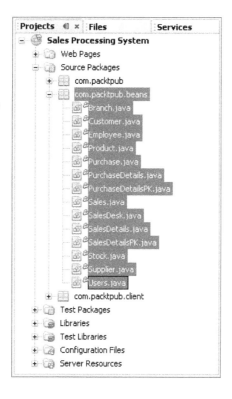

Named query

When the entity classes are generated, we can see the named query annotations followed by the query. This allows us to create a query by just supplying a name for that query. The entity class contains the necessary command for the named query. In the coming example, the query names are `Sales.findAll`, `Sales.findBySalesNo`, and so on, which allow us to find entities easily using these names. We will see later how to use the named queries.

Entity classes

The following is the code for the `Sales` entity class. You can download this source code along with other entity classes from the Packt website.

Just see that based on the `Sales` table in our database, the attributes are declared in this class. In order to set values to these attributes and retrieve the values from these attributes, we have the `set` and `get` methods. Some constructors are also defined. Besides these, the variables are annotated for mapping between the database tables and the entity classes. Some named queries are also generated for the ease of making a query just by using the mentioned name. We will use the generated entity classes in *Chapter 7, Communicating with the Server using GWT RPC* for further processing.

Sales.java

The code for `Sales.java` is as follows:

```java
package com.packtpub.beans;

import java.io.Serializable;
import java.util.Date;
import java.util.List;
import javax.persistence.Basic;
import javax.persistence.CascadeType;
import javax.persistence.Column;
import javax.persistence.Entity;
import javax.persistence.GeneratedValue;
import javax.persistence.GenerationType;
import javax.persistence.Id;
import javax.persistence.JoinColumn;
import javax.persistence.ManyToOne;
import javax.persistence.NamedQueries;
import javax.persistence.NamedQuery;
import javax.persistence.OneToMany;
import javax.persistence.Table;
import javax.persistence.Temporal;
import javax.persistence.TemporalType;

/**
 *
```

```
 * @author Shamsuddin
 */
@Entity
@Table(name = "sales")
@NamedQueries(
{
  @NamedQuery(name = "Sales.findAll",
    query = "SELECT s FROM Sales s"),
  @NamedQuery(name = "Sales.findBySalesNo",
    query = "SELECT s FROM Sales s WHERE s.salesNo = :salesNo"),
  @NamedQuery(name = "Sales.findBySalesDate",
    query = "SELECT s FROM Sales s
    WHERE s.salesDate = :salesDate")
})
/*
```

See the preceding code; the query name is `Sales.findAll`, and the query is `SELECT s FROM Sales s`. When we need such a query, we will just use this name `Sales.findAll`, that will be passed to the Entity Manager.

```
*/
public class Sales implements Serializable {
  private static final long serialVersionUID = 1L;
  @Id
  @GeneratedValue(strategy = GenerationType.IDENTITY)
  @Basic(optional = false)
  @Column(name = "SalesNo")
  private Integer salesNo;
  @Basic(optional = false)
  @Column(name = "SalesDate")
  @Temporal(TemporalType.DATE)
  private Date salesDate;
  @JoinColumn(name = "SalesDeskId",
    referencedColumnName = "SalesDeskId")
  @ManyToOne(optional = false)
  private SalesDesk salesDesk;
  @JoinColumn(name = "EmployeeId",
    referencedColumnName = "EmployeeId")
  @ManyToOne(optional = false)
  private Employee employee;
  @JoinColumn(name = "CustomerNo",
   referencedColumnName = "CustomerNo")
  @ManyToOne
  private Customer customer;
  @OneToMany(cascade = CascadeType.ALL, mappedBy = "sales")
```

```java
      private List<SalesDetails> salesDetailsList;

      /* Some constructors are defined below */

      public Sales()
      {
      }

      public Sales(Integer salesNo)
      {
        this.salesNo = salesNo;
      }

      public Sales(Integer salesNo, Date salesDate)
      {
        this.salesNo = salesNo;
        this.salesDate = salesDate;
      }

   // All getters and setters

      public Integer getSalesNo()
      {
        return salesNo;
      }

      public void setSalesNo(Integer salesNo)
      {
        this.salesNo = salesNo;
      }

      public Date getSalesDate()
      {
        return salesDate;
      }

      public void setSalesDate(Date salesDate)
      {
        this.salesDate = salesDate;
      }

      public SalesDesk getSalesDesk()
      {
        return salesDesk;
      }

      public void setSalesDesk(SalesDesk salesDesk)
      {
        this.salesDesk = salesDesk;
      }

      public Employee getEmployee()
```

```
  {
    return employee;
  }
  public void setEmployee(Employee employee)
  {
    this.employee = employee;
  }
  public Customer getCustomer()
  {
    return customer;
  }
  public void setCustomer(Customer customer)
  {
    this.customer = customer;
  }
  public List<SalesDetails> getSalesDetailsList()
  {
    return salesDetailsList;
  }
  public void setSalesDetailsList(List<SalesDetails> salesDetailsList)
  {
    this.salesDetailsList = salesDetailsList;
  }
  @Override
  public int hashCode()
  {
    int hash = 0;
    hash += (salesNo != null ? salesNo.hashCode() : 0);
    return hash;
  }
  @Override
  public boolean equals(Object object)
  {
    // TODO: Warning - this method won't work in the case the id
fields are not set
    if (!(object instanceof Sales))
    {
      return false;
    }
    Sales other = (Sales) object;
    if ((this.salesNo == null && other.salesNo != null) || (this.
salesNo != null && !this.salesNo.equals(other.salesNo)))
```

```
    {
      return false;
    }
    return true;
  }
  @Override
  public String toString()
  {
    return "com.packtpub.beans.Sales[salesNo=" + salesNo + "]";
  }
}
```

If we recall, we saw that `Sales` and `SalesDetail` have a one-to-many relationship in our database. Because of this, in the entity classes, the `Sales` entity class contains a list of `SalesDetails` (that is many `SalesDetails`), and the `SalesDetails` contains one `Sales` instance (that is one `Sales`).

SalesDetails.java

The following is the code for `SalesDetails.java`:

```
package com.packtpub.beans;

import java.io.Serializable;
import javax.persistence.Basic;
import javax.persistence.Column;
import javax.persistence.EmbeddedId;
import javax.persistence.Entity;
import javax.persistence.JoinColumn;
import javax.persistence.ManyToOne;
import javax.persistence.NamedQueries;
import javax.persistence.NamedQuery;
import javax.persistence.Table;

/**
 *
 * @author Shamsuddin
 */
@Entity
@Table(name = "sales_details")
@NamedQueries(
{
  @NamedQuery(name = "SalesDetails.findAll",
    query = "SELECT s FROM SalesDetails s"),
  @NamedQuery(name = "SalesDetails.findBySalesNo",
    query = "SELECT s FROM SalesDetails s
    WHERE s.salesDetailsPK.salesNo = :salesNo"),
```

```java
    @NamedQuery(name = "SalesDetails.findByProductCode",
      query = "SELECT s FROM SalesDetails s
      WHERE s.salesDetailsPK.productCode = :productCode"),
    @NamedQuery(name = "SalesDetails.findBySalesQuantity",
      query = "SELECT s FROM SalesDetails s
      WHERE s.salesQuantity = :salesQuantity"),
    @NamedQuery(name = "SalesDetails.findByUnitSalesPrice",
      query = "SELECT s FROM SalesDetails s
      WHERE s.unitSalesPrice = :unitSalesPrice")
})
public class SalesDetails implements Serializable {
  private static final long serialVersionUID = 1L;
  @EmbeddedId
  protected SalesDetailsPK salesDetailsPK;
  @Basic(optional = false)
  @Column(name = "SalesQuantity")
  private int salesQuantity;
  @Basic(optional = false)
  @Column(name = "UnitSalesPrice")
  private double unitSalesPrice;
  @JoinColumn(name = "ProductCode", referencedColumnName =
    "ProductCode", insertable = false, updatable = false)
  @ManyToOne(optional = false)
  private Product product;
  @JoinColumn(name = "SalesNo", referencedColumnName = "SalesNo",
    insertable = false, updatable = false)
  @ManyToOne(optional = false)
  private Sales sales;

  public SalesDetails()
  {
  }

  public SalesDetails(SalesDetailsPK salesDetailsPK)
  {
    this.salesDetailsPK = salesDetailsPK;
  }

  public SalesDetails(SalesDetailsPK salesDetailsPK,
    int salesQuantity, double unitSalesPrice)
  {
    this.salesDetailsPK = salesDetailsPK;
    this.salesQuantity = salesQuantity;
    this.unitSalesPrice = unitSalesPrice;
  }

  public SalesDetails(int salesNo, int productCode)
  {
```

```
      this.salesDetailsPK = new SalesDetailsPK(salesNo, productCode);
    }
    public SalesDetailsPK getSalesDetailsPK()
    {
      return salesDetailsPK;
    }
    public void setSalesDetailsPK(SalesDetailsPK salesDetailsPK)
    {
      this.salesDetailsPK = salesDetailsPK;
    }
    public int getSalesQuantity()
    {
      return salesQuantity;
    }
    public void setSalesQuantity(int salesQuantity)
    {
      this.salesQuantity = salesQuantity;
    }
    public double getUnitSalesPrice()
    {
      return unitSalesPrice;
    }
    public void setUnitSalesPrice(double unitSalesPrice)
    {
      this.unitSalesPrice = unitSalesPrice;
    }
    public Product getProduct()
    {
      return product;
    }
    public void setProduct(Product product)
    {
      this.product = product;
    }
    public Sales getSales()
    {
      return sales;
    }
    public void setSales(Sales sales)
    {
      this.sales = sales;
```

```
    }

    @Override
    public int hashCode()
    {
      int hash = 0;
      hash += (salesDetailsPK != null ? salesDetailsPK.hashCode() : 0);
      return hash;
    }

    @Override
    public boolean equals(Object object)
    {
      // TODO: Warning - this method won't work in the case the id
fields are not set
      if (!(object instanceof SalesDetails))
      {
        return false;
      }
      SalesDetails other = (SalesDetails) object;
      if ((this.salesDetailsPK == null && other.salesDetailsPK != null)
        || (this.salesDetailsPK != null &&
        !this.salesDetailsPK.equals(other.salesDetailsPK)))
      {
        return false;
      }
      return true;
    }

    @Override
    public String toString()
    {
      return "com.packtpub.beans.SalesDetails[salesDetailsPK=" +
        salesDetailsPK + "]";
    }
  }
```

SalesDetailsPK is created, as we have the composite primary key in the SalesDetails table. Each of salesNo and productCode is a part of the composite key. SalesDetails entity class contains one instance of SalesDetailsPK.

SalesDetailsPK.java

The code for SalesDetailsPK.java is as follows:

```
package com.packtpub.beans;

import java.io.Serializable;
import javax.persistence.Basic;
```

```java
import javax.persistence.Column;
import javax.persistence.Embeddable;
/**
 *
 * @author Shamsuddin
 */
@Embeddable
public class SalesDetailsPK implements Serializable {
  @Basic(optional = false)
  @Column(name = "SalesNo")
  private int salesNo;
  @Basic(optional = false)
  @Column(name = "ProductCode")
  private int productCode;

  public SalesDetailsPK()
  {
  }

  public SalesDetailsPK(int salesNo, int productCode)
  {
    this.salesNo = salesNo;
    this.productCode = productCode;
  }

  public int getSalesNo()
  {
    return salesNo;
  }

  public void setSalesNo(int salesNo)
  {
    this.salesNo = salesNo;
  }

  public int getProductCode()
  {
    return productCode;
  }

  public void setProductCode(int productCode)
  {
    this.productCode = productCode;
  }

  @Override
  public int hashCode()
  {
```

```
    int hash = 0;
     hash += (int) salesNo;
     hash += (int) productCode;
     return hash;
  }

  @Override
  public boolean equals(Object object)
  {
     // TODO: Warning - this method won't work in the case the id
  fields are not set
     if (!(object instanceof SalesDetailsPK))
     {
       return false;
     }
     SalesDetailsPK other = (SalesDetailsPK) object;
     if (this.salesNo != other.salesNo)
     {
       return false;
     }
     if (this.productCode != other.productCode)
     {
       return false;
     }
     return true;
  }

  @Override
  public String toString()
  {
     return "com.packtpub.beans.SalesDetailsPK[salesNo=" + salesNo +
       ", productCode=" + productCode + "]";
  }
}
```

Creating controller classes

Controller classes are used to simply manage/control the entities. Controller classes create the entity manager and use that manger to create, edit, delete, and find entities.

Getting ready

All the entity classes should be created before going to create the controller classes.

How to do it...

1. Go to **File | New File...**.

2. Select **Sales Processing System** from **Project** drop-down list.

3. Select **Persistence** from the **Categories** list.

4. Select **JPA Controller Classes from Entity Classes** from the **File Types** list, as shown in the following screenshot:

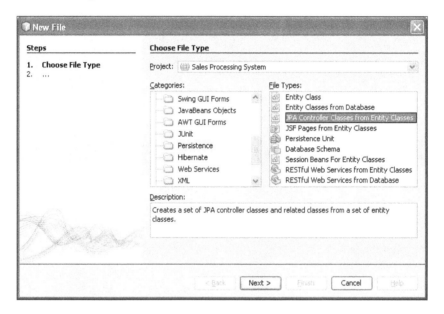

5. Click on **Next**.

6. Add all the available entity classes, except `PurchaseDetails` and `SalesDetails`.

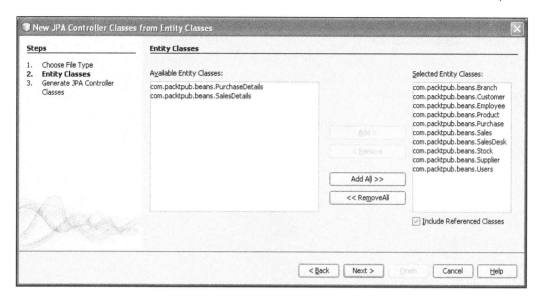

7. Click on **Next**.

8. Give **com.packtpub.controller** as the **Package**, as shown in the following screenshot:

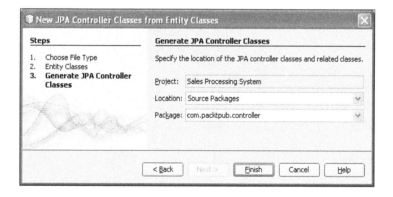

9. Click on **Finish**.

How it works...

The steps we just executed create the JPA controller classes in the **com.packtpub.controller** package, and some exception classes in the **com.packtpub.controller.exceptions** package, as shown in the following screenshot:

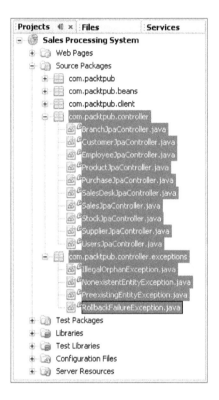

Entity manager

The entity manager is used with the persistence context that manages the life cycle of the entity instances. The entity manager defines the methods that are used to add, remove, or edit entities, find entities by primary key, and query on entities. Some methods are `persist`, `merge`, `remove`, `find`, and so on.

Entity manager factory

The entity manager factory is used to create the entity manager for an application. The code `Persistence.createEntityManagerFactory("Sales Processing SystemPU")` creates an instance of the entity manager factory. Here, the `createEntityManagerFactory` method of the `Peristence` class takes the persistence unit name as its argument.

Controller class for sales entity

The following code is the one for `controller` class for the `Sales` entity. You can download the code for all of the controller class from Packt website. Let's have a look at the `controller` class for the `Sales` entity. This class contains the following operations:

- ▶ Creating the entity manager factory
- ▶ Creating the entity manager
- ▶ Persisting a `Sales` entity
- ▶ Editing a `Sales` entity
- ▶ Deleting a `Sales` entity
- ▶ Finding different `Sales` entities

Importing packages

The following bit of code imports the various packages required:

```
import com.packtpub.beans.Sales;
import com.packtpub.controller.exceptions.IllegalOrphanException;
import com.packtpub.controller.exceptions.NonexistentEntityException;
import javax.persistence.EntityManager;
import javax.persistence.EntityManagerFactory;
import javax.persistence.Persistence;
import javax.persistence.Query;
import javax.persistence.EntityNotFoundException;
import javax.persistence.criteria.CriteriaQuery;
import javax.persistence.criteria.Root;
import com.packtpub.beans.SalesDesk;
import com.packtpub.beans.Employee;
import com.packtpub.beans.Customer;
import com.packtpub.beans.SalesDetails;
import java.util.ArrayList;
import java.util.List;
```

Defining a constructor

Here, the constructor creates the instance of `EntityManagerFactory`, which is a class-level variable, and is used to create the entity manager. This is carried out using the following code:

```
private EntityManagerFactory emf = null;

public SalesJpaController()
{
  emf = Persistence.createEntityManagerFactory
    ("Sales Processing SystemPU");
}
```

Creating the entity manager

The `getEntityManager` method invokes the method `createEntityManager` of `EntityManagerFactory` to return the `EntityManager` instance, as in the following code:

```
public EntityManager getEntityManager()
{
  return emf.createEntityManager();
}
```

Defining a method to persist object

The `controller` class has a method, `create`, that accepts a `Sales` object as the parameter to persist this object. This method constructs the complete `Sales` object and persists (that is, saves) the `Sales` object by invoking the `persist` method of the entity manager. We will see the use of this method in chapter 7. However, let's see some code snippets here:

```
em = getEntityManager();
em.getTransaction().begin();
```

The preceding code creates the `EntityManager` object em, which is a local variable. Then, the transaction is started:

```
Customer customer = sales.getCustomer();
if (customer != null)
{
  customer = em.getReference(customer.getClass(),
    customer.getCustomerNo());
  sales.setCustomer(customer);
}
```

A `Sales` entity has a relation with one instance of `Customer`. The above code gets the instance of `Customer`, whose state may be lazily fetched. That instance is then set in the `Sales` object. Thus, all the other related entities, like `SalesDesk` and `Employee`, are set in the `Sales` object. This is required to update the state of the `Customer`, `Employee`, and `SalesDesk` instances when a new `Sales` entity is added.

Again, a `Sales` entity has many `SalesDetails`. That's why, a list of `SalesDetails` is managed within the `Sales` instance. In the code below, a loop is used to add all the `SalesDetails` objects in a list, which is then set in the `Sales` object:

```
List<SalesDetails> attachedSalesDetailsList =
  new ArrayList<SalesDetails>();
for (SalesDetails salesDetailsListSalesDetailsToAttach :
  sales.getSalesDetailsList())
{
  salesDetailsListSalesDetailsToAttach =
    em.getReference(salesDetailsListSalesDetailsToAttach.getClass(),
```

```
            salesDetailsListSalesDetailsToAttach.getSalesDetailsPK());
        attachedSalesDetailsList.add
            (salesDetailsListSalesDetailsToAttach);
    }
    sales.setSalesDetailsList(attachedSalesDetailsList);
```

Now, the `Sales` object is ready to persist. This is done by the following code:

```
    em.persist(sales);
```

When the `Sales` object is persisted, the state of the other related entities too needs to be updated. The following code updates the `Customer` entity by invoking the `merge` method. The other entities are also updated in the same way, as shown in the following code:

```
    if (customer != null)
    {
        customer.getSalesList().add(sales);
        customer = em.merge(customer);
    }
```

Then, the transaction is committed:

```
    em.getTransaction().commit();
```

At last, the entity manager is closed.

Defining a method to edit object

To update the `Sales` object, a method `edit` is defined in the `controller` class. This method edits the attributes of the `Sales` instance and calls the `merge` method of the entity manager to update a `Sales` object. We will see the use of this method in chapter 7. The entity manager is created first in the same way as shown above. Then, it finds the `Sales` entity in the persistence context. All the other related entities are set and merged as we saw in the preceding code.

Defining method to remove object

To remove an object from the persistence context, a method `destroy` is defined in the `controller` class. This method calls the `remove` method of the entity manager and passes the ID of the object to be removed. We will see the use of this method in chapter 7 as well.

This method does the following sequentially:

- Creates the `EntityManager` object, starting the transaction
- Gets the `Sales` object from the persistence context
- `Sales` is removed from all the other related entities like `Employee`, `Customer`, and `SalesDesk`
- All the other related entities are updated (that is, merged)
- `Sales` is removed from the persistence context
- The transaction is committed

Defining methods for finding objects

There are several methods for finding objects. We can find all the Sales objects in a context, or even a particular Sales object(s). The following code finds a particular Sales object when its ID is given. The find method of EntityManager (called by the em object) takes two parameters: the first one is the Entity class and the second one is the primary key of that entity:

```
public Sales findSales(Integer id)
{
  EntityManager em = getEntityManager();
  try
  {
    return em.find(Sales.class, id);
  } finally
  {
    em.close();
  }
}
```

7
Communicating with the Server using GWT RPC

In this chapter, we will cover:

- ▶ Creating DTO classes
- ▶ Mapping entity classes and DTOs
- ▶ Creating a GWT RPC service
- ▶ Defining an RPC method to persist an object
- ▶ Calling an RPC method from a client UI
- ▶ Finding an entity
- ▶ Updating an entity
- ▶ Deleting an entity
- ▶ Managing a list for RPC
- ▶ Authenticating a user through username and password

Introduction

The Graphical User Interface (GUI) we have created so far resides in the client side of the application. This chapter introduces the communication between the server and the client, where the client (GUI) will send a request to the server, and the server will respond accordingly. In GWT, the interaction between the server and the client is made through the RPC mechanism. **RPC** stands for **Remote Procedure Call**. The concept is that there are some methods in the server side, which are called by the client at a remote location. The client calls the methods by passing the necessary arguments, and the server processes them, and then returns back the result to the client. GWT RPC allows the server and the client to pass Java objects back and forth.

RPC has the following steps:

1. **Defining the GWTService interface**: Not all the methods of the server are called by the client. The methods which are called remotely by the client are defined in an interface, which is called GWTService.

2. **Defining the GWTServiceAsync interface**: Based on the GWTService interface, another interface is defined, which is actually an asynchronous version of the GWTService interface. By calling the asynchronous method, the caller (the client) is not blocked until the method completes the operation.

3. **Implementing the GWTService interface**: A class is created where the abstract method of the GWTService interface is overridden.

4. **Calling the methods**: The client calls the remote method to get the server response.

Creating DTO classes

In this application, the server and the client will pass Java objects back and forth for the operation. For example, the `BranchForm` will request the server to persist a `Branch` object, where the `Branch` object is created and passed to server by the client, and the server persists the object in the server database. In another example, the client will pass the `Branch` ID (as an `int`), the server will find the particular `Branch` information, and then send the `Branch` object to the client to be displayed in the branch form. So, both the server and client need to send or receive Java objects. We have already created the JPA entity classes and the JPA controller classes to manage the entity using the Entity Manager. But the JPA class objects are not transferable over the network using the RPC. JPA classes will just be used by the server on the server side. For the client side (to send and receive objects), DTO classes are used. **DTO** stands for **Data Transfer Object**. DTO is simply a transfer object which encapsulates the business data and transfers it across the network.

Getting ready

Create a package `com.packtpub.client.dto`, and create all the DTO classes in this package.

How to do it...

The steps required to complete the task are as follows:

1. Create a class `BranchDTO` that implements the `Serializable` interface:

   ```
   public class BranchDTO implements Serializable
   ```

2. Declare the attributes. You can copy the attribute declaration from the entity classes. But in this case, do not include the annotations:

   ```
   private Integer branchId;
   private String name;
   private String location;
   ```

3. Define the constructors, as shown in the following code:

   ```
   public BranchDTO(Integer branchId, String name, String location)
   {
     this.branchId = branchId;
     this.name = name;
     this.location = location;
   }
   public BranchDTO(Integer branchId, String name)
   {
     this.branchId = branchId;
     this.name = name;
   }
   public BranchDTO(Integer branchId)
   {
     this.branchId = branchId;
   }
   public BranchDTO()
   {
   }
   ```

 To generate the constructors automatically in NetBeans, right-click on the code, select **Insert Code | Constructor**, and then click on **Generate** after selecting the attribute(s).

4. Define the getter and setter:

```
public Integer getBranchId()
{
   return branchId;
}
public void setBranchId(Integer branchId)
{
   this.branchId = branchId;
}
public String getLocation()
{
   return location;
}
public void setLocation(String location)
{
   this.location = location;
}
public String getName()
{
   return name;
}
public void setName(String name)
{
   this.name = name;
}
```

 To generate the setter and getter automatically in NetBeans, right-click on the code, select **Insert Code | Getter and Setter...**, and then click on **Generate** after selecting the attribute(s).

Mapping entity classes and DTOs

In RPC, the client will send and receive DTOs, but the server needs pure JPA objects to be used by the Entity Manager. That's why, we need to transform from DTO to JPA entity class and vice versa. In this recipe, we will learn how to map the entity class and DTO.

Getting ready

Create the entity and DTO classes.

How to do it...

1. Open the `Branch` entity class and define a constructor with a parameter of type `BranchDTO`. The constructor gets the properties from the DTO and sets them in its own properties:

    ```
    public Branch(BranchDTO branchDTO)
    {
      setBranchId(branchDTO.getBranchId());
      setName(branchDTO.getName());
      setLocation(branchDTO.getLocation());
    }
    ```

2. This constructor will be used to create the `Branch` entity class object from the `BranchDTO` object.

3. In the same way, the `BranchDTO` object is constructed from the entity class object, but in this case, the constructor is not defined. Instead, it is done where it is required to construct DTO from the entity class.

There's more...

Some third-party libraries are available for automatically mapping entity class and DTO, such as Dozer and Gilead. For details, you may visit `http://dozer.sourceforge.net/` and `http://noon.gilead.free.fr/gilead/`.

Creating the GWT RPC Service

In this recipe, we are going to create the GWTService interface, which will contain an abstract method to add a `Branch` object to the database.

Getting ready

Create the `Branch` entity class and the DTO class.

How to do it...

The steps are as follows:

1. Go to **File** | **New File...**.
2. Select **Google Web Toolkit** from **Categories** and **GWT RPC Service** from **File Types**, as shown in the following screenshot:

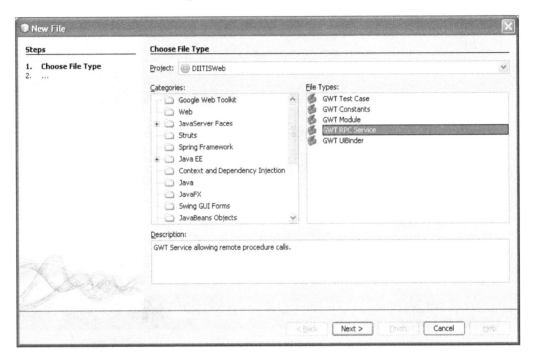

3. Click on **Next**.
4. Give **GWTService** as the **Service Name**.
5. Give **rpc** as the **Subpackage** (this is optional), as shown in the following screenshot:

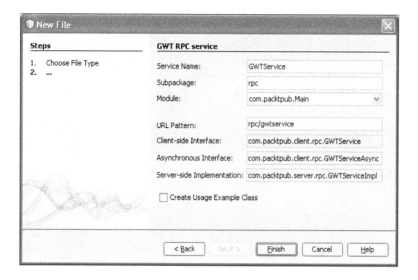

6. Click on **Finish**.

How it works...

A total of three classes are created, which are com.packtpub.client.rpc.GWTService,
com.packtpub.client.rpc.GWTServiceAsync, and com.packtpub.server.rpc.
GWTServiceImple. Note that GWTService is created in the client-side package, and the
implementation class is in the server package. Because of the preceding steps, the following
code is generated:

```java
// GWTService.java
package com.packtpub.client.rpc;
import com.google.gwt.user.client.rpc.RemoteService;
import com.google.gwt.user.client.rpc.RemoteServiceRelativePath;

// This is the servlet mapping in web.xml file
@RemoteServiceRelativePath("rpc/gwtservice")
public interface GWTService extends RemoteService
{
  public String myMethod(String s);
}

// GWTServiceAsync.java
package com.packtpub.client.rpc;
import com.google.gwt.user.client.rpc.AsyncCallback;
public interface GWTServiceAsync
{
  public void myMethod(String s, AsyncCallback<String> callback);
}
```

```
// GWTServiceImpl.java
package com.packtpub.server.rpc;
import com.google.gwt.user.server.rpc.RemoteServiceServlet;
import com.packtpub.client.rpc.GWTService;
public class GWTServiceImpl extends RemoteServiceServlet
  implements GWTService
{
  public String myMethod(String s)
  {
    // Do something interesting with 's' here on the server.
    return "Server says: " + s;
  }
}
```

The GWTService interface will include a signature of all the methods which will be called remotely. NetBeans automatically creates a dummy method to understand the concept of RPC. Observe that the myMethod method has no body here; it just has the header part.

An asynchronous version of this method is declared in the GWTServiceAsync interface. The significant changes are:

- ▸ The return type, String, is changed to void
- ▸ A new parameter of type AsyncCallback is added

This is because the asynchronous method returns the value through the AsyncCallback object passed to the method as argument.

In addition, the GWTServiceImpl includes implementation of the method.

Defining an RPC method to persist objects

In this recipe, we are going to:

- ▸ Declare an abstract method add in the GWTService interface
- ▸ Declare an abstract asynchronous method add in GWTServiceAsync interface
- ▸ Implement the method in the GWTServiceImpl class

This method will take BranchDTO as a parameter, and add the BranchDTO object in the database.

Getting ready

GWTService, GWTServiceAsync interface, and GWTServiceImpl must be created first.

How to do it...

1. Open GWTService.java and add the following code:

    ```java
    public boolean add(BranchDTO branchDTO);
    ```

2. Open GWTServiceAsync.java and add the following code:

    ```java
    public void add(BranchDTO branchDTO,
        AsyncCallback<java.lang.Boolean> asyncCallback);
    ```

3. Open GWTServiceImpl.java and add the following code:

    ```java
    @Override
    public boolean add(BranchDTO branchDTO)
    {
      Branch branch = new Branch();
      branch.setBranchId(branchDTO.getBranchId());
      branch.setName(branchDTO.getName());
      branch.setLocation(branchDTO.getLocation());

      BranchJpaController branchJpaController = new
    BranchJpaController();
      boolean added=false;
      try
      {
        branchJpaController.create(branch);
        added=true;
      }
      catch (PreexistingEntityException ex)
      {
        Logger.getLogger(GWTServiceImpl.class.getName()).
          log(Level.SEVERE, null, ex);
      }
      catch (Exception ex)
      {
        Logger.getLogger(GWTServiceImpl.class.getName()).
          log(Level.SEVERE, null, ex);
      }
      return added;
    }
    ```

How it works...

Here, we have created a method add to persist a Branch object. As a pure JPA entity class is not transferable through RPC, we have taken the BranchDTO object as a parameter. Then, the JPA entity class is constructed from the DTO class.

Constructing the JPA entity class from the DTO needs just the following steps:

1. Creating an instance of the JPA entity class (over here, `Branch`).

2. Get the properties from the DTO class and set them in the JPA entity class.

After constructing the JPA entity class, the instance of the controller class is created as the controller class contains the necessary methods to persist, update, delete, find, and so on operations. A Boolean variable added is used to track the success of the operation. The variable added is initialized to `false` and set to `true` when the persist operation is completed successfully. The `create` method of the controller class persists the object.

Calling the RPC method from Client UI

In this recipe, we will call the RPC method from the file `BranchForm`. This method will be called when the **Save** button is clicked.

How to do it...

1. Open the file `BranchForm.java` and create the `AsyncCallback` instance as follows:

```
final AsyncCallback<Boolean> callback =
  new AsyncCallback<Boolean>()
{
  MessageBox messageBox = new MessageBox();
  @Override
  public void onFailure(Throwable caught)
  {
    messageBox.setMessage("An error occured!
      Cannot save Branch information");
    messageBox.show();
  }

  @Override
  public void onSuccess(Boolean result)
  {
    if (result)
    {
      messageBox.setMessage("Branch information saved
        successfully");
    } else
    {
      messageBox.setMessage("An error occured!
        Cannot save Branch information");
    }
    messageBox.show();
  }
};
```

2. Write the event-handling code for the "add" button, as in the following code. Here, the `branchDTO` is a class-level instance of `BranchDTO`.

```
saveButton.addSelectionListener(new
  SelectionListener<ButtonEvent>() {
  @Override
  public void componentSelected(ButtonEvent ce)
  {
    branchDTO=new BranchDTO();
    branchDTO.setBranchId(Integer.parseInt
      (branchIdField.getValue()));
    branchDTO.setName(nameField.getValue());
    branchDTO.setLocation(locationField.getValue());
    ((GWTServiceAsync) GWT.create(GWTService.class)) .
      add(branchDTO, callback);
  }
});
```

3. Run the application, open the Branch Form, and enter the input, as shown in the following screenshot:

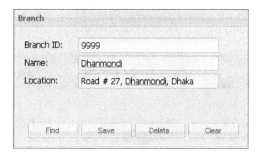

4. Click on the **Save** button. A confirmation message is shown, as in the following screenshot:

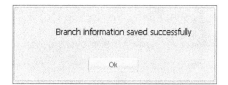

How it works...

Let's now see the aspects in some detail:

- **Creating an** `AsyncCallback` **instance**: The first step to call the RPC method is to create an instance of the `AsyncCallback` interface because the result from the server is sent to the client through this instance. The `AsyncCallback` interface contains the following two abstract methods:

  - `onSuccess`: This method is called automatically when the operation can be run successfully in the server side. This method has a parameter according to the type of the result the server sends. In our case, this type is Boolean, as we will get the result as `true` or `false` after the add operation.

  - `onFailure`: If the RPC method cannot be invoked for any reason, this method is called automatically. Generally, the error messages are shown from this method.

- **Calling the** `RPC` **method**: This part handles the calling portion of the RPC method. Here, we have constructed the `BranchDTO` object and have called the `add` method of the GWTServiceAsync interface. The GWTServiceAsync object is created by the `create` method of GWT class. Notice that the `AsyncCallback` object is passed to the `add` method, and we receive the result in this object.

Finding an entity

In this recipe, we are going to write the code to find an entity. From the client side, the ID of the entity will be passed to the server; the server will find the entity in the database using the JPA controller class, and then return the entity to the client in order to display it.

How to do it...

1. Declare the following method in the GWTService interface:

   ```
   public BranchDTO findBranch(int branchId);
   ```

2. Declare the asynchronous version of the above method in GWTServiceAsync interface

   ```
   public void findBranch(int branchId, AsyncCallback<BranchDTO>
   asyncCallback);
   ```

3. Implement this method in GWTServiceImpl class

   ```
   @Override
   public BranchDTO findBranch(int branchId)
   {
     Branch branch=branchJpaController.findBranch(branchId);
     BranchDTO branchDTO=null;
   ```

```
if(branch!=null)
{
  branchDTO=new BranchDTO();
  branchDTO.setBranchId(branch.getBranchId());
  branchDTO.setName(branch.getName());
  branchDTO.setLocation(branch.getLocation());
}
return branchDTO;
}
```

4. Create a callback instance in client side (`BranchForm` in this case) to call this method as shown in the following code:

```
final AsyncCallback<BranchDTO> callbackFind =
  new AsyncCallback<BranchDTO>()
{
  @Override
  public void onFailure(Throwable caught)
  {
    MessageBox messageBox = new MessageBox();
    messageBox.setMessage("An error occured!
      Cannot complete the operation");
    messageBox.show();
    clear();
  }
  @Override
  public void onSuccess(BranchDTO result)
  {
    branchDTO=result;
    if(result!=null)
    {
      branchIdField.setValue(""+branchDTO.getBranchId());
      nameField.setValue(branchDTO.getName());
      locationField.setValue(branchDTO.getLocation());
     }
    else
    {
      MessageBox messageBox = new MessageBox();
      messageBox.setMessage("No such Branch found");
      messageBox.show();
      clear();
    }
  }
};
```

5. Write the event-handling code for the `find` button as follows:

```
findButton.addSelectionListener(new
  SelectionListener<ButtonEvent>()
  {
    @Override
    public void componentSelected(ButtonEvent ce)
    {
    MessageBox inputBox = MessageBox.prompt("Input",
      "Enter the Branch ID");
    inputBox.addCallback(new Listener<MessageBoxEvent>()
    {
      public void handleEvent(MessageBoxEvent be)
      {
        int branchId = Integer.parseInt(be.getValue());
        ((GWTServiceAsync)GWT.create(GWTService.class)).
          findBranch(branchId,callbackFind);
      }
    });
    }
  });
```

How it works...

Here, the steps for calling the RPC method are the same as we had done for the add/save operation. The only difference is the type of the result we have received from the server. We have passed the `int` branch ID and have received the complete `BrachDTO` object, from which the values are shown in the branch form.

Updating an entity

In this recipe, we are going to write the code to update an entity. The client will transfer the DTO of updated object, and the server will update the entity in the database using the JPA controller class.

How to do it...

1. Declare the following method in the GWTService interface:

   ```
   public boolean updateBranch(BranchDTO branchDTO);
   ```

2. Declare the asynchronous version of this method in the GWTServiceAsync interface:

   ```
   public void updateBranch(BranchDTO branchDTO,
     AsyncCallback<java.lang.Boolean> asyncCallback);
   ```

3. Implement the method in the GWTServiceImpl class:

```
@Override
public boolean updateBranch(BranchDTO branchDTO)
{
  boolean updated=false;
  try
  {
    branchJpaController.edit(new Branch(branchDTO));
    updated=true;
  }
  catch (IllegalOrphanException ex)
  {
  Logger.getLogger(GWTServiceImpl.class.getName()).
    log(Level.SEVERE, null, ex);
  }
  catch (NonexistentEntityException ex)
  {
    Logger.getLogger(GWTServiceImpl.class.getName()).
      log(Level.SEVERE, null, ex);
  }
  catch (Exception ex)
  {
    Logger.getLogger(GWTServiceImpl.class.getName()).
      log(Level.SEVERE, null, ex);
  }
  return updated;
}
```

4. Create a callback instance for this method in the client side (BranchForm in this case, if it is not created yet):

```
final AsyncCallback<Boolean> callback =
  new AsyncCallback<Boolean>()
{
  MessageBox messageBox = new MessageBox();
  @Override
  public void onFailure(Throwable caught)
  {
    messageBox.setMessage("An error occured!
      Cannot complete the operation");
    messageBox.show();
  }
  @Override
  public void onSuccess(Boolean result)
  {
```

```
       if (result)
       {
         messageBox.setMessage("Operation completed successfully");
       } else
       {
         messageBox.setMessage("An error occured!
           Cannot complete the operation");
       }
       messageBox.show();
     }
   };
```

5. Write the event handle code for the update button:

```
updateButton.addSelectionListener(new
  SelectionListener<ButtonEvent>()
{
  @Override
  public void componentSelected(ButtonEvent ce)
  {
    branchDTO.setName(nameField.getValue());
    branchDTO.setLocation(locationField.getValue());
    ((GWTServiceAsync)GWT.create(GWTService.class)).
      updateBranch(branchDTO,callback);
    clear();
  }
});
```

How it works...

This operation is also almost the same as the `add` operation shown previously. The difference here is the method of controller class. The method `edit` of the controller class is used to update an entity.

Deleting an entity

In this recipe, we are going to write the code to delete an entity. The client will transfer the ID of the object, and the server will delete the entity from the database using the JPA controller class.

How to do it...

1. Declare the following method in the GWTService interface

```
public boolean deleteBranch(int branchId);
```

2. Declare the asynchronous version of this method in GWTServiceAsync interface

```
public void deleteBranch(int branchId,
  AsyncCallback<java.lang.Boolean> asyncCallback);
```

3. Implement the method in GWTServiceImpl class

```
@Override
public boolean deleteBranch(int branchId)
{
  boolean deleted=false;
  try
  {
    branchJpaController.destroy(branchId);
    deleted=true;
  }
  catch (IllegalOrphanException ex)
  {
    Logger.getLogger(GWTServiceImpl.class.getName()).
      log(Level.SEVERE, null, ex);
  }
  catch (NonexistentEntityException ex)
  {
    Logger.getLogger(GWTServiceImpl.class.getName()).
      log(Level.SEVERE, null, ex);
  }
  return deleted;
}
```

4. Create a callback instance for this method in the client side (BranchForm in this case, if it is not created yet):

```
final AsyncCallback<Boolean> callback = new
  AsyncCallback<Boolean>()
{
  MessageBox messageBox = new MessageBox();

  @Override
  public void onFailure(Throwable caught)
  {
    messageBox.setMessage("An error occured!
      Cannot complete the operation");
    messageBox.show();
  }

  @Override
  public void onSuccess(Boolean result)
  {
    if (result)
```

```
        {
          messageBox.setMessage("Operation completed successfully");
        } else
        {
          messageBox.setMessage("An error occured!
            Cannot complete the operation");
        }
        messageBox.show();
      }
    };
```

5. Write the event handling code for the delete button:

```
deleteButton.addSelectionListener(new
  SelectionListener<ButtonEvent>()
{
  @Override
  public void componentSelected(ButtonEvent ce)
  {
    ((GWTServiceAsync)GWT.create(GWTService.class)).
      deleteBranch(branchDTO.getBranchId(),callback);
    clear();
  }
});
```

How it works...

A detailed explanation of the steps can be found in the previous recipes. For deleting an entity, the `destroy` method of the controller class is called.

Managing a list for RPC

Sometimes, we need to transfer a list of objects as `java.util.List` (or a collection) back and forth between the server and the client. We already know from the preceding recipes that the JPA entity class objects are not transferable directly using RPC. Because of the same reason, any list of the JPA entity class is not transferable directly. To transfer `java.util.List` using RPC, the list must contain objects from DTO classes only. In this recipe, we will see how we can manage a list for RPC.

In our scenario, we can consider two classes—Customer and Sales. The association between these two classes is that one customer makes zero or more sales and one sale is made by one customer. Because of such an association, the customer class contains a list of sales, and the sales class contains a single instance of customer class. For example, we want to transfer the full customer object with the list of sales made by this customer. Let's see how we can make that possible.

How to do it...

1. Create DTO classes for `Customer` and `Sales` (`CustomerDTO` and `SalesDTO`, respectively) as shown in the first recipe of this chapter. In the following table, the required changes in data types are shown for the entity and DTO class attributes. The list in the DTO class contains objects of only the DTO class; on the other hand, the list of the entity class contains objects of entity class.

Class	Entity class attributes	DTO class attributes
Customer	`Integer customerNo;`	`Integer customerNo;`
	`String name;`	`String name;`
	`String address;`	`String address;`
	`String contactNo;`	`String contactNo;`
	`List<Sales> salesList`	`List<SalesDTO> salesDTOList;`
Sales	`Integer salesNo;`	`Integer salesNo;`
	`Date salesDate;`	`Date salesDate;`
	`SalesDesk salesDesk;`	`SalesDeskDTO salesDeskDTO;`
	`Employee employee;`	`EmployeeDTO employeeDTO;`
	`Customer customer;`	`CustomerDTO customerDTO;`
	`List<SalesDetails> salesDetailsList;`	`List<SalesDetailsDTO> salesDetailsDTOList;`

2. Define the following constructor in the `Customer` entity class:

```
public Customer(CustomerDTO customerDTO)
{
  setCustomerNo(customerDTO.getCustomerNo());
  setName(customerDTO.getName());
  setAddress(customerDTO.getAddress());
  setContactNo(customerDTO.getContactNo());

  List<SalesDTO> salesDTOList=customerDTO.getSalesList();
  salesList = new ArrayList<Sales>();
  for(int i=0;i<salesDTOList.size();i++)
  {
    SalesDTO salesDTO=salesDTOList.get(i);
    Sales sales=new Sales(salesDTO);
    salesList.add(sales);
  }
}
```

3. Define the following constructor in the `Sales` entity class:

```
public Sales(SalesDTO salesDTO)
{
  setSalesNo(salesDTO.getSalesNo());
  setSalesDate(salesDTO.getSalesDate());
  setCustomer(new Customer(salesDTO.getCustomer()));
  // there's more but not relevant for this recipe
}
```

How it works...

Now in the server side, the entity classes, `Customer` and `Sales`, will be used, and in the client side, `CustomerDTO` and `SalesDTO`, will be used. Constructors with DTO class type argument are defined for the mapping between entity class and DTO class. To recall this, refer to the *Mapping entity classes and DTOs* recipe.

But here, the addition is the loop used for creating the list. From the `CustomerDTO` class, we get a list of `SalesDTO`. The loop gets one `SalesDTO` from the list, converts it to `Sales`, and adds it in the `Sales` list—that's all.

See also

▸ The *Creating DTO classes* recipe
▸ The *Mapping entity classes and DTOs* recipe

Authenticating a user through username and password

In this recipe, we are going to create the necessary methods to authenticate a user through a login process.

Getting ready

Create the DTO class for the entity class `Users`.

How to do it...

1. Declare the following method in the GWTService interface:

```
public UsersDTO login(String username,String password);
```

2. Declare the following method in the GWTServiceAsync interface:

```
public void login(String username, String password,
  AsyncCallback<UsersDTO> asyncCallback);
```

3. Implement the method in the GWTServiceImpl class:

```
@Override
public UsersDTO login(String username, String password)
{
  UsersDTO userDTO = null;
  UsersJpaController usersJpaController =
    new UsersJpaController();
  Users user = (Users) usersJpaController.findUsers(username);
  if (user != null)
  {
    if (user.getPassword().equals(password))
    {
      userDTO=new UsersDTO();
      userDTO.setUserName(user.getUserName());
      userDTO.setPassword(user.getPassword());
      EmployeeDTO employeeDTO=
        new EmployeeDTO(user.getEmployee().getEmployeeId());
      employeeDTO.setName(user.getEmployee().getName());
      userDTO.setEmployeeDTO(employeeDTO);
    }
  }
  return userDTO;
}
```

How it works...

A username and password are passed to the method. An object of the UsersJpaController class is created to find the Users object based on the given username. If the find method returns null, it means that no such user exists. Otherwise, the password of the Users object is compared with the given password. If both the passwords match, a UsersDTO object is constructed and returned.

The client will call this method during the login process. If the client gets null, the client should handle it accordingly, as the username/password is not correct. If it is not null, the user is authenticated.

8
Reporting with iReport

In this chapter, we will cover:

- ▶ Installing iReport plugins in NetBeans
- ▶ Creating reports
- ▶ Adding parameters in reports
- ▶ Adding subreports
- ▶ Adding variables
- ▶ Showing reports in GWT as HTML
- ▶ Creating `HtmlReportViewer`
- ▶ Calling `HtmlReportViewer`
- ▶ Showing reports in GWT as `PDF`
- ▶ Creating `PdfReportViewer`
- ▶ Calling `PdfReportViewer`

Introduction

iReport is the most popular open source reporting tool for Java. The motivation to use iReport in a GWT application is that it will provide an easy-to-create and a good-looking report output in HTML, PDF, or any other suitable format in the information systems developed in GWT.

Important features

 ▶ Report wizard to develop reports easily and quickly

 ▶ Support for parameterized report, master-detail report using the subreport feature, crosstab report, and charting

 ▶ iReport plugins for NetBeans to design reports from inside the NetBeans IDE

Installing iReport plugins in NetBeans

In this recipe, we are going to install the following iReport plugins, which will enable us to create reports from inside the NetBeans IDE. We are installing the version 3.7.0. The plugins are:

 ▶ `iReport-3.7.0.nbm`

 ▶ `jasperreports-components-plugin-3.7.0.nbm`

 ▶ `jasperreports-extensions-plugin-3.7.0.nbm`

 ▶ `jasperserver-plugin-3.7.0.nbm`

Getting ready

Download the plugins from `http://jasperforge.org//website/ireportwebsite/IR%20Website/ir_download.html?header=project&target=ireport`.

How to do it...

Following are the steps required to complete the task:

1. Start NetBeans IDE.
2. Go to the **Tools** menu and click on **Plugins | Downloaded**.
3. Click on the **Add Plugins...** button.
4. Browse, select, and open the plugins.

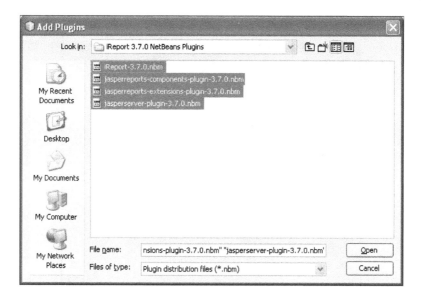

5. Select all of the listed plugins and click on **Install**.

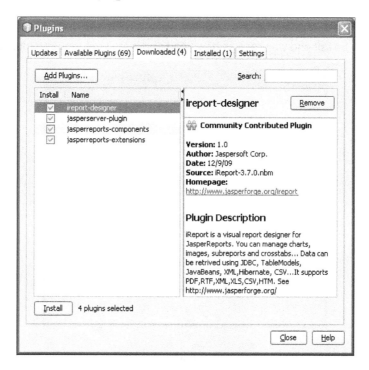

6. Click on **Next**.

7. Click on **Next**, and then click on **Accept** to accept the terms in the license agreement.

8. Click on **Install** and wait for it to download and install the required plugins:

9. Click on **Finish** to complete the installation.

How it works...

After installing the plugins, the following file types will be available in NetBeans under **Report** categories:

- ▶ **Empty report**
- ▶ **Empty Report (using Groovy for expressions)**
- ▶ **Report Wizard**
- ▶ **Style Template**
- ▶ **Chart Theme**
- ▶ **Resource Bundle**

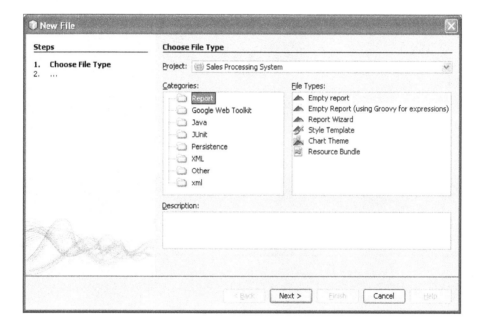

Creating a report

In this recipe, we are going to create a report that shows the list of sales.

How to do it...

1. Go to **File** | **New File...**.
2. Select **Report** from **Categories** and **Report Wizard** from **File Types**.

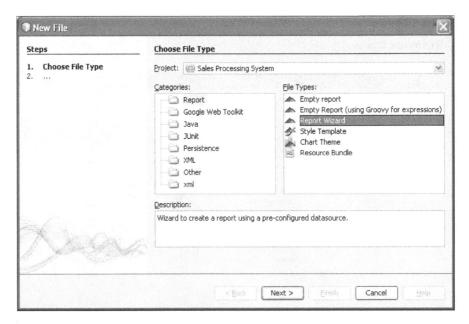

3. Click on **Next**.
4. Select **Simple Blue** from **Layout**:

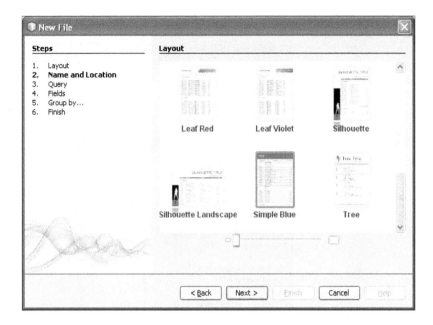

5. Enter **Sales.jrxml** as the **File Name**, and type in **Reports** as the **Folder**:

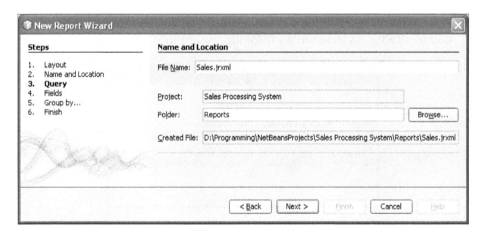

6. Click on **Next**.
7. Click on the **New** button to create a new connection.

8. Select **NetBeans Database JDBC Connection** as the datasource type:

9. Enter **Sales** for **Name** and select **jdbc:mysql://localhost:3306/Sales** from the **Connection** list, as shown in the following screenshot:

10. Click on **Save**.

11. Click on **Design Query**.

12. Double-click on the **Employee**, **Sales**, and **Customer** tables.

13. Select **SalesNo**, **SalesDate**, and **SalesDeskID** from **Sales**; **EmployeeId** and **Name** from **Employee**; **CustomerNo** and **Name** from **Customer**:

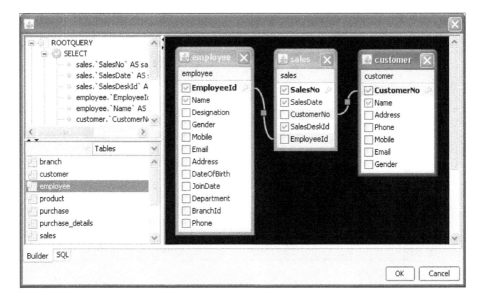

14. Click on **OK**.

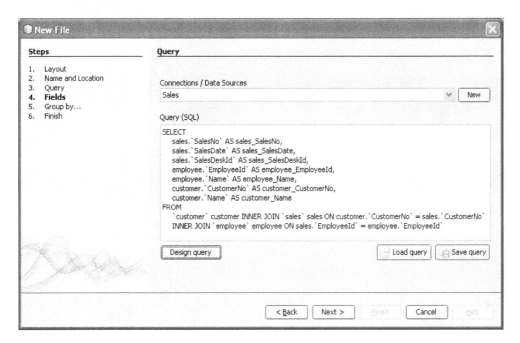

15. Click on **Next** and select all the fields:

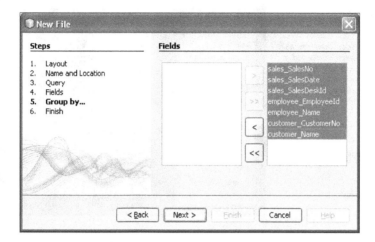

16. Click on **Next**, and then again click on **Next** without selecting any group.
17. Click on **Finish**.
18. Change the **Title** to **Sales Invoice**, remove the data from the **Add a description here** field, and drag and drop the fields to rearrange them as follows:

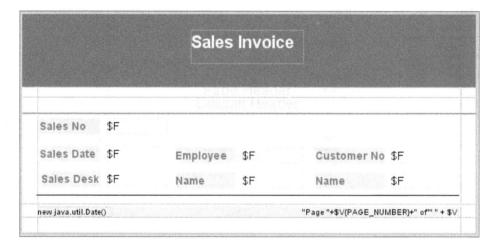

19. Preview the report:

How it works...

The preceding steps have created a `.jrxml` file in the `Reports` folder of the NetBeans project. Using the NetBeans Database JDBC Connection, a connection is established with the database to retrieve the metadata and the data while previewing the report. Selecting tables and fields in Design Query creates an SQL command. In our case, the following SQL command is created.

```
SELECT
  sales.`SalesNo` AS sales_SalesNo,
  sales.`SalesDate` AS sales_SalesDate,
  sales.`SalesDeskId` AS sales_SalesDeskId,
  employee.`EmployeeId` AS employee_EmployeeId,
  employee.`Name` AS employee_Name,
  customer.`CustomerNo` AS customer_CustomerNo,
  customer.`Name` AS customer_Name
FROM
  `customer` customer INNER JOIN `sales` sales ON customer.`CustomerNo`
    = sales.`CustomerNo`
  INNER JOIN `employee` employee ON sales.`EmployeeId` =
    employee.`EmployeeId`
```

Writing this code manually (without using Design Query) will give the same result. Sometimes, we may also prefer writing the query directly.

When the wizard is finished, we need to modify the reports, especially the title and column names. The wizard creates columns according to the SQL command, but we need to change them to appropriate text that is displayable to the user.

Adding a parameter in a report

In the previous recipe, we created a report which shows all the sales record, but mostly we need to show only a particular sales record. For this reason, we need to filter the data. Generally, to filter SQL data, we write a WHERE clause in the SQL command. To filter the data here, we need to pass a value to the report. Thus, the data depending on the passed value will be shown. In most cases, the value of a primary key is passed to the report through a parameter.

Parameters are a type of report objects used just to pass data to the report engine. The data may be passed from another report or from any program, or directly from the user. That passed data is then used for filling the report dynamically. Actually, parameters act like dynamic filters in the query that supplies data for the report.

Getting ready

Create the report as shown in the previous recipe.

How to do it...

1. Click on the **Report Inspector** tab on the left-hand side of the **Report designer** tab.
2. Right-click on **Parameters** and click on **Add Parameter....**

3. On the right-hand side, the **Parameter** properties will appear. Set the following properties:

 ❑ **Name**: **salesNo**

 ❑ **Parameter Class**: **java.lang.Integer**

 ❑ **Use as a prompt** : **Selected**

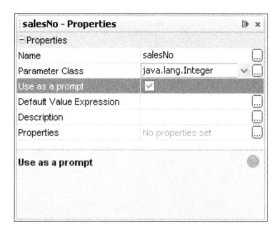

4. Click on the **Report query** toolbar icon at the top of the report designer. In the **Report query** dialog, add the following WHERE clause at the end of the SQL command:

```
WHERE
    sales.`SalesNo` = $P{salesNo}
```

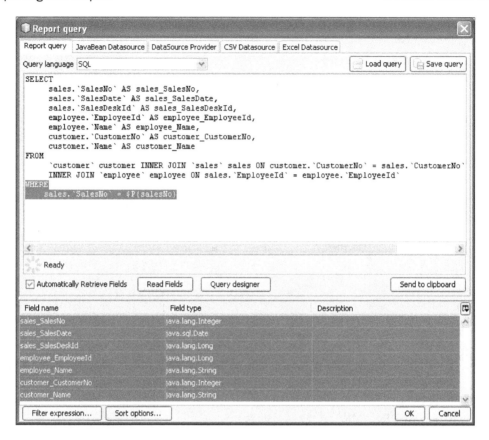

5. Click on **OK**.
6. Preview the report and enter **1** for **salesNo**:

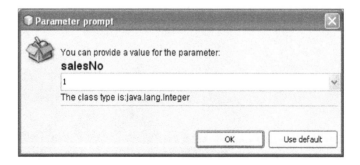

7. The report will now show filtered data (only for **Sales No 1**):

Sales Invoice

Sales No	1					
Sales Date	16/08/2010	Employee	1	Customer No	1	
Sales Desk	4	Name	Saiful Islam	Name	Jashim Uddin	

How it works...

The steps we just followed have added a parameter named `salesNo`. Parameter data type (`Parameter Class`) depends on the attribute type of the database table. Here, the type of the `salesNo` attribute in the `Sales` table is `Integer`; that's why we have chosen `java.lang.Integer` as the `Parameter Class`. In the `WHERE` clause of the SQL command, `$P` stands for `Parameter`, and `salesNo` within the curly braces is the parameter name which you give when you add a parameter.

Adding a subreport

In the previous report, we have shown the sales number, sales date, sales desk number, ID, and name, of both the employee and the customer. Now, we want to show the sales details (product ID, name, quantity, and price) at the bottom of the reports. For this, we have to create another report showing the sales details, and we want to see the output of that report at the bottom of the sales data shown in the report prepared in the previous recipe. To show the output of a report inside another report, a subreport is used.

A subreport is an entire report which is placed in another report. If you have one item that is linked to several items in another table, such as a sales report containing sales details, then a subreport is what you need. In such a case, generally the main report (where the subreport is placed) contains the data of the **master/parent** table, and the subreport contains the data of the **detail/child** table. For example, one "Sales table" has many "Sales_Details" tables, where "Sales" is the master/parent table, and "Sales_Details" is the detail/child table. In our database, if we want to show the details of a particular sale, then in the main report, we will show the sale number, the sales date, the employee information, and the customer information, and in the subreport, we will show the product information, the quantity, the price, and so on.

Note that a subreport can be used for many other purposes also and not just for printing records of a child table. We can show the output of a report in another report by using the subreport feature of iReport.

The process for creating a subreport is almost similar to creating a normal report. A subreport has most of the characteristics of a normal report. The difference is that a subreport is placed as an object inside a report.

Typically, a subreport is used:

- To combine master and detail data
- To combine unrelated reports into a single report
- To link two reports
- To present different aspects of the same data

Getting ready

Create the report as shown in the previous recipe.

How to do it...

1. Open the file `Sales.jrxml`, increase the height of the detail band, and decrease the size of the column header and the page header (using your mouse):

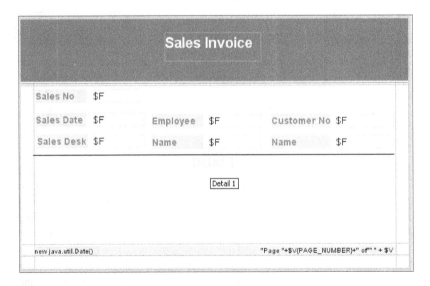

2. Drag the **Subreport** element from **Palette | Report Elements** and drop it on the detail band:

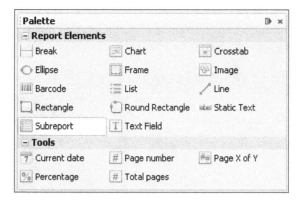

3. The **Subreport wizard** will open. In the first step of the subreport wizard, select **Create a new report**, and then click on **Next**:

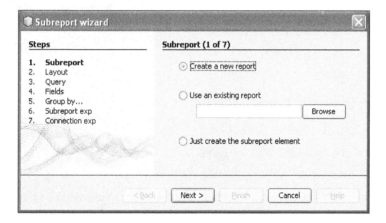

4. Select **Simple Blue** from the **Layout** and click on **Next**.
5. Select **Sales** from the **Connection** list.

6. Open **Design Query** and select **product** and **sales_details** table by double-clicking on them. Select **ProductCode** and **Name** from the **product** table, and **SalesQuantity** and **UnitSalesPrice** from the **sales_details** table, as shown in the following screenshot:

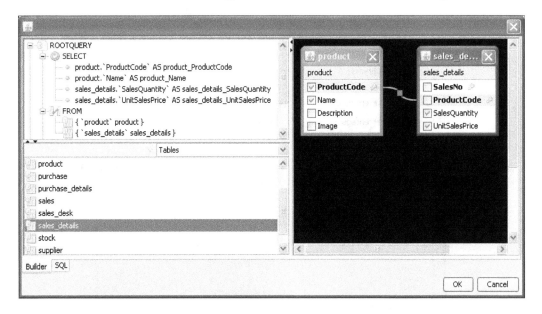

7. Click on **OK**, and then click on **Next**.

8. Select all the fields and click on **Next**.

9. Click on **Next** again without selecting any group.

10. In the step 6 of the subreport wizard (that is the step **Subreport exp**, as seen in the following screenshot), select **Use a static absolute path reference**:

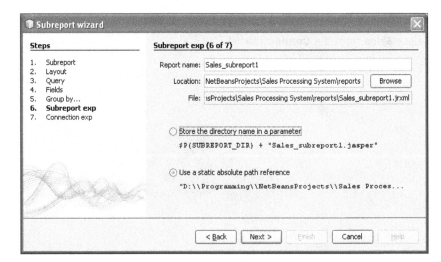

11. Click on **Next**.

12. In the last step of the subreport wizard (**Connection exp**), select **Use the same connection used to fill the master report**, and then click on **Finish**.

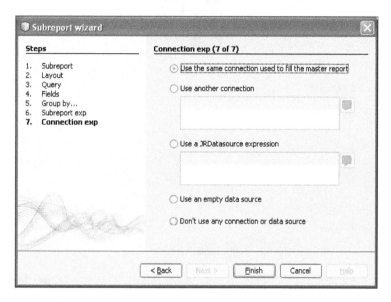

13. Report designer for the subreport now appears:

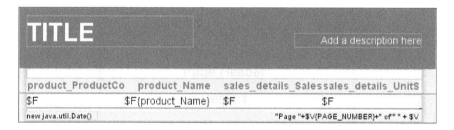

14. Remove all elements from the **Title** and **Page Footer** bands.

15. Set the band height to **0** (zero) for the **Title**, **Page Header**, and **Page Footer** bands. Change the column header appropriately. The design should look similar to the following screenshot:

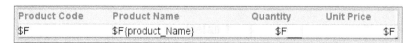

16. Create a parameter for **salesNo** and modify the query appropriately.

17. Compile the subreport.

18. Design of the master report looks as shown in the following screenshot:

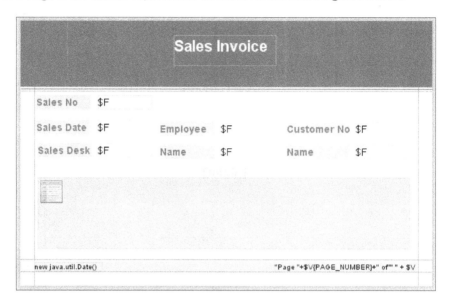

19. Select the subreport elements in the master report, go to the **Properties** window, scroll down to **Parameters**, and click on the **Parameters** button.

20. Click on **Copy From Master** in the **Parameters** dialog:

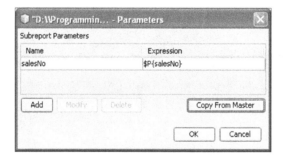

21. Click on **OK**.

22. Preview the master report and input **1** for **salesNo**:

Sales Invoice

Sales No	1				
Sales Date	16/08/2010	Employee	1	Customer No	1
Sales Desk	4	Name	Saiful Islam	Name	Jashim Uddin

Product Code	Product Name	Quantity	Unit Price
1	Beauty Soap	2	30.0
2	Shampoo	1	135.0
3	Baby Milk	1	395.0
5	Bread	4	25.0
8	Chanachur	1	40.0

How it works...

There are two parts in the report. The first part is the master part and the second part is the detail part, which is the subreport here. An important thing here is filtering the data—data in the master part is filtered according to the user input (sales number). Also, the value of this sales number is passed to the detail part to filter the data in the detail report; this was done using the **Copy From Master** button.

Adding a variable

In the previous recipes, we retrieved data from the database and just viewed those after designing the report. However, we haven't done any other processing using the retrieved data. Sometimes, we may need further processing of data. For example, we have retrieved the quantity and unit price of all products of a particular sale; now we might want to calculate the total by multiplying quantity and unit price. We may also want to calculate the grand total (add all totals) of that sale. Please note that the total and the grand total are not stored in the database. We want to calculate these during the runtime of the report. Variables are used in such cases.

In iReport, the report variable is a special object for a report which holds a value during the runtime of the report based on the expression and other setups (Reset Type, Reset Group, Increment Type, Increment Group, and so on).

Getting ready

The subreport created in the previous recipe will be used here to add variables.

How to do it...

1. Go to the **Report Inspector**, right-click on **Variables**, and select **Add Variable**:

2. The **Properties** window for this variable appears on the right-hand side of the design window. Set the following properties:

Name	Value
Name	total
Variable Class	java.lang.Double
Variable Expression	new java.lang.Double ($F{sales_details_SalesQuantity}.intValue()*$F{sales_details_UnitSalesPrice}.doubleValue())

Leave the other properties as set by default.

3. Drag the variable total listed under **Variables** in the **Report Inspector**, drop this on the report, and re-arrange the elements in the report, as shown in the following screenshot:

Product CodeProduct Name		Quantity	Unit Price	Total
$F	$F{product_Name}	$F	$F	$V{total}

4. Preview the report and you'll see the output, as follows:

Product Code	Product Name	Quantity	Unit Price	Total
1	Beauty Soap	2	30.0	60.0
2	Shampoo	1	135.0	135.0
3	Baby Milk	1	395.0	395.0
5	Bread	4	25.0	100.0
8	Chanachur	1	40.0	40.0

5. Now, we will add the **grandTotal** variable that sums up all the totals. In the same way, create new variables and set their properties as below:

Name	Value
Name	grandTotal
Variable Class	java.lang.Double
Calculation	Sum
Variable Expression	$V{total}

6. The summary band is invisible now, as its height is zero. Select the **Summary** band in the **Report Inspector** and set **25** as the **Height** in the **Properties** window.

7. Drag and drop the **grandTotal** variable at the bottom of the total and in the **Summary** band, as shown in the following screenshot. Add static text just before the variable:

Product Code	Product Name	Quantity	Unit Price	Total
$F	$F{product_Name}	$F	$F	$V{total}
			Grand Total	$V{grandTotal}

8. Preview the report and see the output as shown in the following screenshot:

Sales Invoice

Sales No	1					
Sales Date	16/08/2010	Employee	1	Customer No	1	
Sales Desk	4	Name	Saiful Islam	Name	Jashim Uddin	

Product Code	Product Name	Quantity	Unit Price	Total
1	Beauty Soap	2	30.0	60.0
2	Shampoo	1	135.0	135.0
3	Baby Milk	1	395.0	395.0
5	Bread	4	25.0	100.0
8	Chanachur	1	40.0	40.0
			Grand Total	730.0

How it works...

When we add a variable, it works based on the set properties. Generally in the properties window, we name a variable, choose a data type, select **Calculation** if we want to use the built-in function, and write the variable expression. In the previous example, we have chosen `java.lang.Double` as the `Variable Class Type` (data type).

For the variable `total`, we have not used any built-in function because we will multiply two fields—quantity and unit price. The variable `expression new java.lang.Double` `($F{sales_details_SalesQuantity}.intValue()*$F{sales_details_` `UnitSalesPrice}.doubleValue())` means:

▸ We are creating a `Double` instance

▸ Primitive `int` value is received from the `Integer` field, `$F{sales_details_SalesQuantity}`

▸ Primitive `double` is obtained from `Double` field, `$F{sales_details_UnitSalesPrice}`

▸ The primitive values are multiplied

For `grandTotal`, we have calculated the sum of variables, `$V{total}` by choosing the `Sum` from `Calculation`, and writing `$V{total}` as the `Variable Expression`.

Showing a report in the GWT application as HTML

In this recipe, we are going to create a method that converts a jasper report to HTML. This method will be used when we will want to show the report in HTML format.

Getting ready

We need to add the `JasperReports` library to show reports designed by iReport. The following `.jar` files are needed to be added to the library:

- commons-beanutils-1.8.2
- commons-collections-3.2.1
- commons-lang-2.4
- commons-logging-1.1.1
- iText-2.1.0
- jasperreports-3.7.0
- jcommon-1.0.15

To add these `.jar` files to the library, follow these steps:

1. Create a folder `lib` in the project.
2. Place the `.jar` files in the `lib` folder.
3. Right-click on **Libraries** in the **Project** tab and select **Add Jar/Folder...**:

4. Select and open the `.jar` files from the `lib` folder:

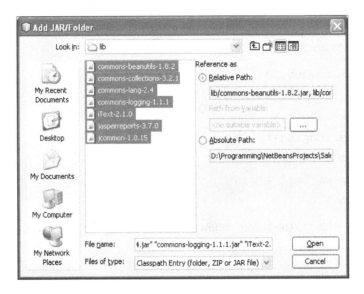

How to do it...

1. Declare the following abstract method in the `GWTService` interface:

```
public String getHtmlReport(String fileName,HashMap<String,Integer> param);
```

2. Declare the asynchronous version of the above method in the `GWTServiceAsync` interface:

```
public void getHtmlReport(String fileName, HashMap<String,Integer> param, AsyncCallback<String> asyncCallback);
```

3. Implement the above method in the `GWTServiceImpl` class:

```
@Override
public String getHtmlReport(String fileName,
  HashMap<String,Integer> param)
{
  try
  {
    InitialContext ctx=new InitialContext();
    DataSource dataSource=(DataSource)ctx.lookup("sales");
    Connection con=dataSource.getConnection();
    String filePath = getServletConfig().getServletContext().
getRealPath(fileName);
    JasperPrint print = JasperFillManager.fillReport(filePath+".
jasper", param, con);
```

```
    String newFileName =  filePath+".html";
    JasperExportManager.exportReportToHtmlFile(print,
newFileName);
    return fileName+".html";
}
catch (NamingException ex)
{
  Logger.getLogger(GWTServiceImpl.class.getName()).
    log(Level.SEVERE, null, ex);
}
catch (SQLException ex)
{
  Logger.getLogger(GWTServiceImpl.class.getName()).
    log(Level.SEVERE, null, ex);
}
catch (JRException ex)
{
  Logger.getLogger(GWTServiceImpl.class.getName()).
    log(Level.SEVERE, null, ex);
}
return null;
}
```

How it works...

Let's see a detailed aspect of this method:

▶ **Parameter**: The method has two parameters. The first one is the jasper report filename, which will be converted to HTML, and the second one is a HashMap object, where the parameters for the report are stored. The parameter name and its value are stored in the HashMap object as a pair.

▶ **Return type**: The method returns the name of the HTML file as String.

▶ **Task description**: The method does the following:

   ❑ Creates an instance of javax.naming.InitialContext:

   ```
   InitialContext ctx=new InitialContext();
   ```

   ❑ Looks up the javax.sql.DataSource object from the InitialContext instance, providing the JNDI name, sales:

   ```
   DataSource dataSource=(DataSource)ctx.lookup("sales");
   ```

   ❑ Creates an instance of the java.sql.Connection from the DataSource object:

   ```
   Connection con=dataSource.getConnection();
   ```

- ❏ The method accepts the relative path of the report (such as `reports\`
  `Sales.jasper`) and converts the relative path to the complete path
  (such as `C:\Program Files\glassfish-3.0.1\glassfish\`
  `domains\domain1\applications\Sales_Processing_System\`
  `reports\Sales.jasper`). This is because the `fillReport` method of
  `JasperFillManager` class (used in the next step) requires the full path of
  the report file:

  ```
  String filePath = getServletConfig().getServletContext().
  getRealPath(fileName);
  ```

- ❏ Invokes the `fillReport` method of `JasperFillManager` that fills the
  report with data, and returns a `JasperPrint` object:

  ```
  JasperPrint print = JasperFillManager.fillReport(filePath+".
  jasper", param, con);
  ```

- ❏ Exports the report to HTML format:

  ```
  JasperExportManager.exportReportToHtmlFile(print,
  newFileName);
  ```

- ❏ The following exceptions must be caught:

  ```
  javax.naming.NamingException
  java.sql.SQLException
  net.sf.jasperreports.engine.JRException
  ```

Creating HTML report viewer

We are going to create a report viewer to show the report created by iReport in the GWT
application. This viewer class will call the method created in the previous recipe.

How to do it...

1. Import the following classes:

   ```
   com.extjs.gxt.ui.client.widget.MessageBox;
   com.extjs.gxt.ui.client.widget.form.FormPanel;
   com.extjs.gxt.ui.client.widget.layout.FitLayout;
   com.google.gwt.core.client.GWT;
   com.google.gwt.user.client.rpc.AsyncCallback;
   com.google.gwt.user.client.ui.Frame;
   com.packtpub.client.rpc.GWTService;
   com.packtpub.client.rpc.GWTServiceAsync;
   java.util.HashMap;
   ```

2. Create class `HtmlReportViewer` by extending the `FormPanel` class:

```
class HtmlReportViewer extends FormPanel
```

3. Define the constructor:

```
public HtmlReportViewer(String fileName, HashMap<String, Integer>
param, String title)
{
  setLayout(new FitLayout());
  setHeading(title);
  final Frame frame = new Frame();
  add(frame);

  AsyncCallback<String> reportURLCallback =
    new AsyncCallback<String>()
  {
    MessageBox messageBox = new MessageBox();

    @Override
    public void onFailure(Throwable caught)
    {
      messageBox.setMessage("Cannot load the report.
        \nCannot connect to remote resource");
      messageBox.show();
      caught.printStackTrace();
    }

    @Override
    public void onSuccess(String result)
    {
      if (result != null)
      {
        frame.setUrl(result);
      }
      else
      {
        messageBox.setMessage("Cannot load the report");
        messageBox.show();
      }
    }
  };
  ((GWTServiceAsync) GWT.create(GWTService.class)).
    getHtmlReport(fileName, param, reportURLCallback);
}
```

How it works...

This class performs the following operations:

▶ Creates and adds a frame inside the panel (this class is a panel, as it extends the `FormPanel` class).

▶ Creates an instance of the `AsyncCallback` class, which is used to call the `getHtmlReport` method. If the call fails, an error message is shown, and if the call succeeds, the URL of the HTML report is set in the frame. The frame then shows the HTML output of the report.

Calling HtmlReportViewer

In this recipe, we will call the viewer (created in the previous recipe) from the user interface when a menu item is clicked.

Getting ready

Ensure that the `HtmlReportViewer` class is created according to the previous recipe.

How to do it...

1. Write the event handling code in the `HomePage` class:

```
salesDetailMenuItem.addListener(Events.Select,new
Listener<MenuEvent>()
{
  @Override
  public void handleEvent(MenuEvent be)
  {
    MessageBox inputBox = MessageBox.prompt
      ("Input", "Enter the Sales No");
    inputBox.addCallback(new Listener<MessageBoxEvent>()
    {
      public void handleEvent(MessageBoxEvent be)
      {
        int salesNo = Integer.parseInt(be.getValue());
        HashMap<String, Integer> param = new HashMap
          <String, Integer>();
        param.put("salesNo", salesNo);
        HtmlReportViewer reportViewer = new HtmlReportViewer
          ("reports/Sales", param, "Sales Invoice");
```

```
        addTab("Sales Detail",reportViewer);
    }
    });
    }
});
```

2. Run the project and click on the **Sales Detail** menu item to view the report as shown in the following screenshot:

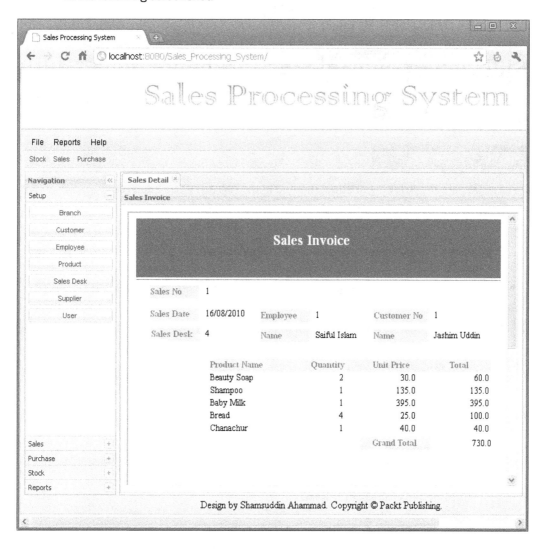

How it works...

As the report will be shown when the user clicks on the **Sales Detail** menu item, the event-handling code is written for the `salesDetailMenuItem` item. Here, we have done the following:

1. We have created the `MessageBox` object to take input (the **Sales No**) from the user.

2. We have created the `HashMap` object to pass the parameter value to the report. We have created the HTML report viewer and added this in the main content panel.

Showing a report in a GWT application as PDF

In this recipe, we are going to create a method that converts a jasper report to PDF. This method will be used when we will want to show the report in PDF format.

How to do it...

1. Declare the following abstract method in the `GWTService` interface:

   ```
   public String getPdfReport(String
     fileName,HashMap<String,Integer> param);
   ```

2. Declare the asynchronous version of the previous method in the `GWTServiceAsync` interface:

   ```
   public void getPdfReport(String fileName, HashMap<String,Integer>
     param, AsyncCallback<String> asyncCallback);
   ```

3. Implement the previous method in the `GWTServiceImpl` class:

   ```
   public String getPdfReport(String fileName, HashMap
     <String,Integer> param)
   {
     try
     {
       Class.forName("com.mysql.jdbc.Driver");
       Connection con = DriverManager.getConnection
         ("jdbc:mysql://localhost:3306/sales", "root", "shams");
       String filePath = getServletConfig().getServletContext().
         getRealPath(fileName);
       JasperPrint print = JasperFillManager.fillReport
         (filePath+".jasper", param, con);
       String newFileName =  filePath+".pdf";
       JasperExportManager.exportReportToPdfFile(print, newFileName);
       return fileName+".pdf";
     }
   ```

```
catch (SQLException ex)
{
  Logger.getLogger(GWTServiceImpl.class.getName()).
    log(Level.SEVERE, null, ex);
}
catch (ClassNotFoundException ex)
{
  Logger.getLogger(GWTServiceImpl.class.getName()).
    log(Level.SEVERE, null, ex);
}
catch (JRException ex)
{
  Logger.getLogger(GWTServiceImpl.class.getName()).
    log(Level.SEVERE, null, ex);
}
return null;
}
```

How it works...

Let's see a detailed aspect of this method:

▶ **Parameter**: This method has two parameters. The first one is the jasper report filename, which will be converted to HTML, and the second one is a `HashMap` object, where the parameters for the report are stored. The parameter name and the value of that parameter are stored in the `HashMap` object as a pair.

▶ **Return type**: The method returns the name of the PDF file as a `string`

▶ **Task description**: The method does the following:

  ❑ Creates an instance of `javax.naming.InitialContext`

    ```
    InitialContext ctx=new InitialContext();
    ```

  ❑ Looks up the `javax.sql.DataSource` object from the `InitialContext` instance providing the JNDI name `sales`.

    ```
    DataSource dataSource=(DataSource)ctx.lookup("sales");
    ```

  ❑ Creates an instance of the `java.sql.Connection` from the `DataSource` object.

    ```
    Connection con=dataSource.getConnection();
    ```

❑ The method accepts the relative path of the report (such as `reports\Sales.jasper`) and converts the relative path to the complete path (such as `C:\Program Files\glassfish-3.0.1\glassfish\domains\domain1\applications\Sales_Processing_System\reports\Sales.jasper`). This is because the `fillReport` method of `JasperFillManager` class(used in the next step) requires the full path of the report file:

```
String filePath = getServletConfig().getServletContext().
getRealPath(fileName);
```

❑ Invokes the `fillReport` method of `JasperFillManager` that fills the report with data, and returns a `JasperPrint` object:

```
JasperPrint print = JasperFillManager.fillReport(filePath+".
jasper", param, con);
```

❑ Exports the report to PDF format:

```
JasperExportManager.exportReportToPdfFile(print,
newFileName);
```

❑ Following exceptions must be caught:

```
javax.naming.NamingException
java.sql.SQLException
net.sf.jasperreports.engine.JRException
```

Creating a PDF report viewer

We are going to create a report viewer to show the report created by iReport in the GWT application. This viewer class will call the method created in the previous recipe.

How to do it...

1. Import the following classes:

```
com.extjs.gxt.ui.client.widget.MessageBox;
com.extjs.gxt.ui.client.widget.form.FormPanel;
com.extjs.gxt.ui.client.widget.layout.FitLayout;
com.google.gwt.core.client.GWT;
com.google.gwt.user.client.rpc.AsyncCallback;
com.google.gwt.user.client.ui.Frame;
com.packtpub.client.rpc.GWTService;
com.packtpub.client.rpc.GWTServiceAsync;
java.util.HashMap;
```

2. Create the `PdfReportViewer` class by extending the `FormPanel` class:

```
class HtmlReportViewer extends FormPanel
```

3. Define the constructor:

```java
public PdfReportViewer(String fileName, HashMap
  <String, Integer> param, String title)
{
  setLayout(new FitLayout());
  setHeading(title);
  final Frame frame = new Frame();
  add(frame);
  AsyncCallback<String> reportURLCallback =
    new AsyncCallback<String>()
  {
    MessageBox messageBox = new MessageBox();
    @Override
    public void onFailure(Throwable caught)
    {
      messageBox.setMessage("Cannot load the report.
        \nCannot connect to remote resource");
      messageBox.show();
      caught.printStackTrace();
    }

    @Override
    public void onSuccess(String result)
    {
      if (result != null)
      {
        frame.setUrl(result);
      } else
      {
        messageBox.setMessage("Cannot load the report");
        messageBox.show();
      }
    }
  };

  ((GWTServiceAsync) GWT.create(GWTService.class)).
  getPdfReport(fileName, param, reportURLCallback);
}
```

How it works...

This class performs the following operations:

- ▶ Creates and adds a frame inside the panel (this class is a panel as it extends the FormPanel class)
- ▶ Creates an instance of the AsyncCallback class, which is used to call the getPdfReport method. If the call fails, an error message is shown, and if the call succeeds, the URL of the PDF report is set in the frame. The frame then shows the PDF output of the report.

Calling PdfReportViewer

In this recipe, we will call the viewer (created in the previous recipe) from the user interface when a menu item is clicked.

Getting ready

Ensure that the PdfReportViewer class is created according to the previous recipe.

How to do it...

1. Write the event-handling code in the HomePage class:

```
salesDetailMenuItem.addListener
  (Events.Select,new Listener<MenuEvent>()
{
  @Override
  public void handleEvent(MenuEvent be)
  {
    MessageBox inputBox = MessageBox.prompt
      ("Input", "Enter the Sales No");
    inputBox.addCallback(new Listener<MessageBoxEvent>()
    {
      public void handleEvent(MessageBoxEvent be)
      {
        int salesNo = Integer.parseInt(be.getValue());
        HashMap<String, Integer> param = new HashMap<String,
          Integer>();
        param.put("salesNo", salesNo);
        PdfReportViewer reportViewer = new PdfReportViewer
          ("reports/Sales", param, "Sales Invoice");
        addTab("Sales Detail",reportViewer);
      }
    });
```

```
    }
});
```

2. Run the project and click on the **Sales Detail** menu item to view the report as shown in the following screenshot:

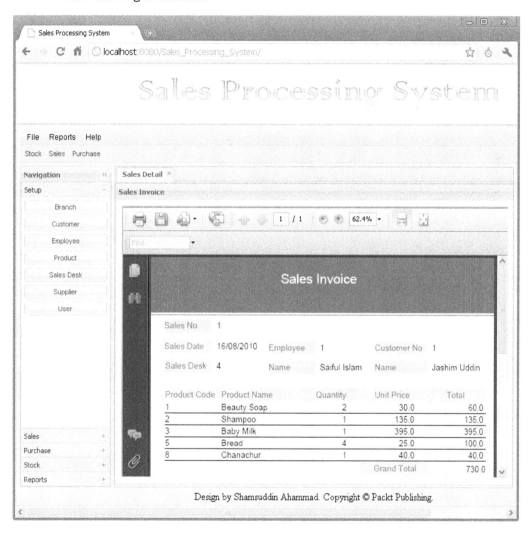

How it works...

As the report will be shown when the user clicks on the **Sales Detail** menu item, the event-handling code is written for the `salesDetailMenuItem`. Here, we have done the following:

- ► We have created the `MessageBox` object to take the **Sales No** input from the user
- ► We have created the `HashMap` object to pass the parameter value to the report
- ► We have created the `PDF` report viewer and added this in the main content panel.

9
Deploying a GWT Application

In this chapter, we will cover:

- ▸ Building a project and creating the WAR file
- ▸ Deploying on the GlassFish Server from NetBeans
- ▸ Creating JDBC Connection Pool in the GlassFish Server
- ▸ Creating JDBC Resource in the GlassFish Server
- ▸ Deploying the WAR file in the GlassFish Server

Introduction

In this chapter, we will work for deployment of the GWT application in the GlassFish Server. Because we have developed the application using NetBeans, we can deploy the application directly from NetBeans. Sometimes, we need to deploy the application by configuring the GlassFish Server manually. In this chapter, we are going to deploy in both the ways—manually, and from NetBeans.

Building a project and creating the WAR file

The building process of the GWT application includes creating the web directory structure, compiling Java files to class files, copying library files, compiling GWT client-side code, and creating the WAR files.

Getting ready

Before starting to deploy, we need to create the WAR file containing all the required project files. "WAR" stands for "Web Application Archive". WAR is a JAR file that contains the Java classes, Java Server Pages, Servlets, library files, static web pages, and so on, as necessary. The WAR file is used to distribute the application files in a single file. In this recipe, we are going to create the WAR file for our GWT application using the NetBeans IDE.

How to do it...

The steps required to complete the task are as follows:

1. Go to **Project Properties | Libraries**.

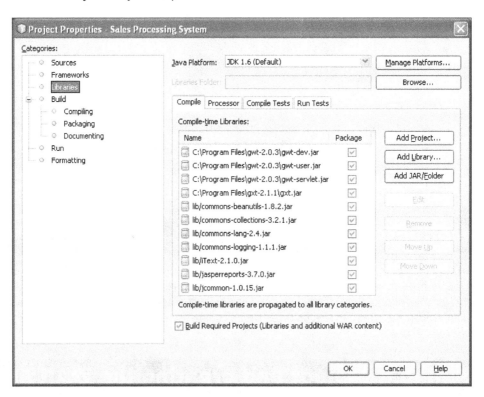

2. Under the **Compile** tab, check all the checkboxes for the files to be packaged, as shown in the previous screenshot.

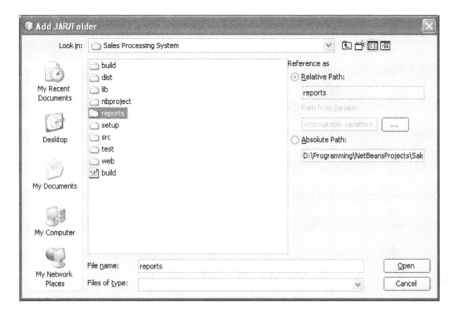

3. Go to **Build | Packaging**, click on **Add File/Folder** button, select and open the **reports** folder (as shown in the previous screenshot), and give **reports** as the **Path in WAR** (as shown in the following screenshot):

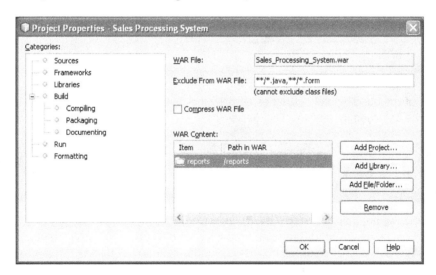

4. Click on **OK**.
5. Go to the **Run** menu and select **Build Main Project**.

How it works...

NetBeans does everything as per the configuration to build the project which creates the WAR file at the end of the build. What **Build Main Project** consists of can be seen from the NetBeans output console. We can see the output as shown in the following screenshot:

At the end of the building process, it has created the `Sales_Processing_System.war` file, which will be deployed in the GlassFish Server.

Deploying on the GlassFish Server from NetBeans

In this recipe, we are going to deploy the application from NetBeans. This means that the application will be deployed to GlassFish from inside the NetBeans IDE. All the necessary server configurations will be carried out by NetBeans. Refer to the following recipes in this chapter to know what server configuration is required.

Getting ready

Build the project completely as shown in the previous recipe.

How to do it...

1. Select the **Sales Processing System** project in the **Project** tab.

2. Right-click on the project name **Sales Processing System**.

3. Select the option **Deploy** from the drop-down menu. After this, the GlassFish Server will start (if it has not started already), and the application will be deployed:

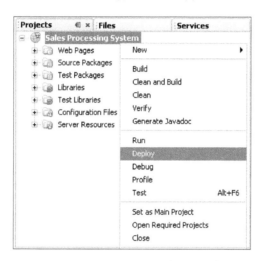

How it works...

NetBeans starts the server and deploys the application in the build\web folder of the project.

The NetBeans console output is shown in the following screenshot:

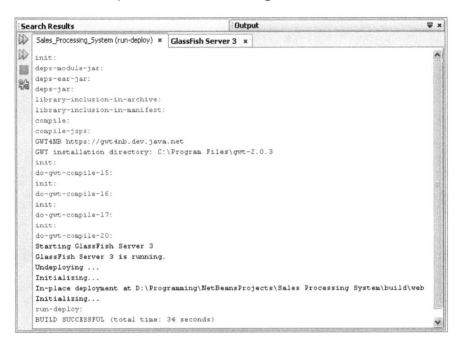

The following screenshot shows the console output of the GlassFish Server:

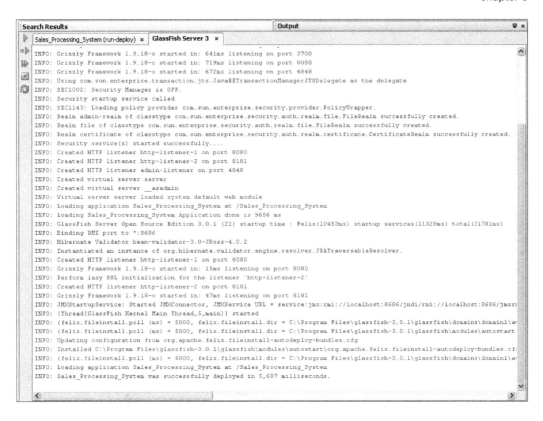

Creating the JDBC Connection Pool in GlassFish

As our application connects with the database, a JDBC Connection Pool needs to be created in the GlassFish Server before deploying the WAR file. When we deploy the application from NetBeans, the connection pool is automatically created by NetBeans, but if we want to deploy from the GlassFish admin console, we need to create the connection pool manually. In this recipe, we are going to see how to create the JDBC Connection Pool from the GlassFish admin console.

Getting ready

Start the GlassFish Server. To start the server, go to the following (or the appropriate) location: `C:\Program Files\glassfish-3.0.1\glassfish\bin`, and execute the `startserv.bat` file, as shown in the following screenshot:

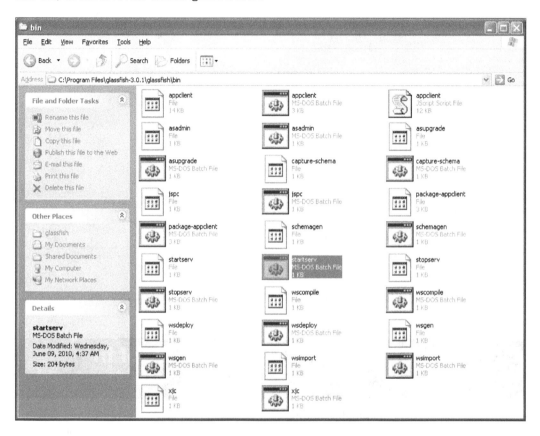

This will start the server. We will see the console output as shown in the following screenshot:

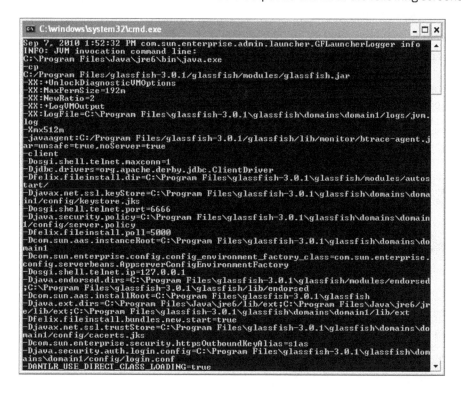

How to do it...

1. Start the browser and go to the address `http://localhost:4848`.

2. Obviously, in most cases, the GlassFish admin console is password-protected, unless you have not provided any password during the installation. Provide the username and password. If the login credentials are correct or the admin console is not password-protected, we are redirected to `http://localhost:4848/common/index.jsf`.

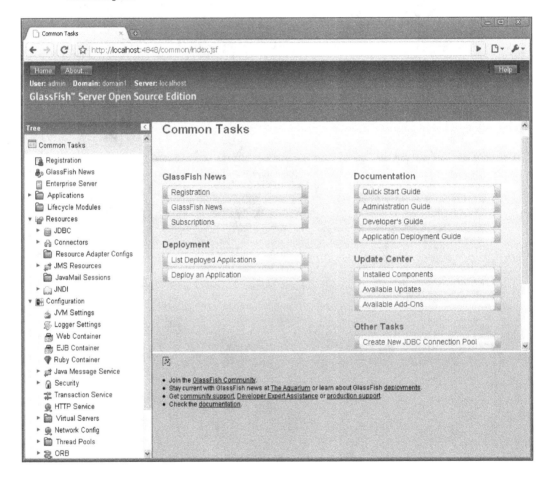

3. From the **Tree** menu on the left-hand side of the admin console, go to **Resources |**
   JDBC | Connection Pools.

4. Click on **Next**.
5. Set the following properties:

Properties	Value
Name	mysql_Sales_rootPool
Resource Type	javax.sql.DataSource
Database Vendor	MySql

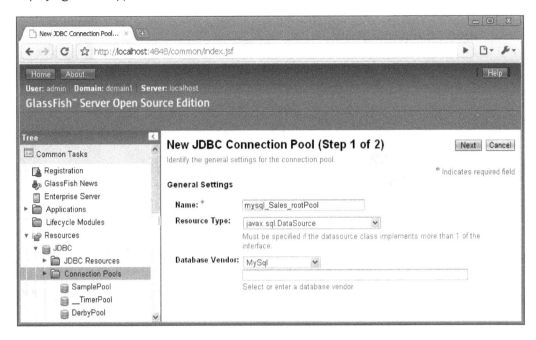

6. Click on **Next**.

7. Scroll down to the **Additional Properties** section and set the following properties:

Name	Value
User	root
PortNumber	3306
DatabaseName	sales
Password	packt
DriverClass	com.mysql.jdbc.Driver
ServerName	localhost
URL	jdbc:mysql://localhost/sales

8. Click on **Finish**.

How it works...

The preceding steps have created a JDBC Connection Pool through which the server gets connected to the database.

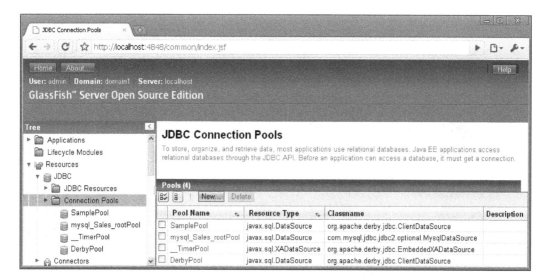

Creating a JDBC Resource in GlassFish Server

In this recipe, we are going to create a JDBC resource which will provide the application a means to connect to a database.

Getting ready

Start the GlassFish server as shown in the previous recipe.

How to do it...

1. Start the **GlassFish Server Administration Console**.

2. From the **Tree** menu on the left-hand side, go to **Resources | JDBC | JDBC Resources**.

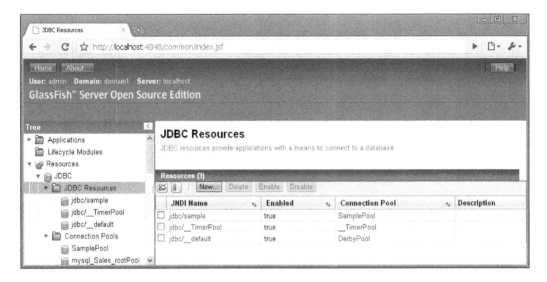

3. Click on the **New** button.

4. Give **sales** as the **JNDI Name**.

5. Select **mysql_Sales_rootPool** from the **Pool Name**, as shown in the following screenshot:

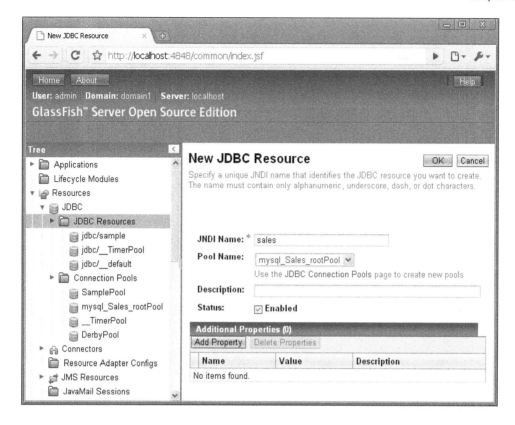

6. Click on **OK**. A JDBC resource in the GlassFish Server is now created:

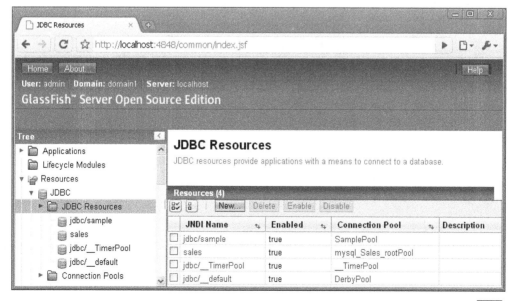

Deploying the WAR file in the GlassFish Server

In this recipe, we will deploy the WAR file, Sales_Processing_System.war, in the GlassFish Server. After the deployment, the user will be able to browse the application.

Getting ready

Build the complete project.

How to do it...

1. Start the **GlassFish Server Administration Console**.
2. From the **Tree** menu, go to **Applications**.

3. Click on the **Deploy** button.
4. Click on the **Choose File** button under **Packaged File to Be Uploaded to the Server**, and select the WAR file Sales_Processing_System.war from the location \ Sales Processing System\dist.

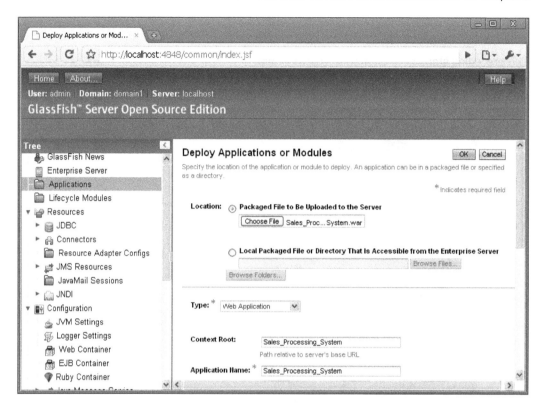

5. Click on **OK** and wait for the processing. If everything is fine, the application will be listed.

6. Click on the **Launch** link under **Action** of the listed applications.

How it works...

The preceding steps have created a directory named Sales_Processing_System within the server at the location C:\Program Files\glassfish-3.0.1\glassfish\ domains\domain1\applications. This directory contains all the necessary project files, as shown in the following screenshot:

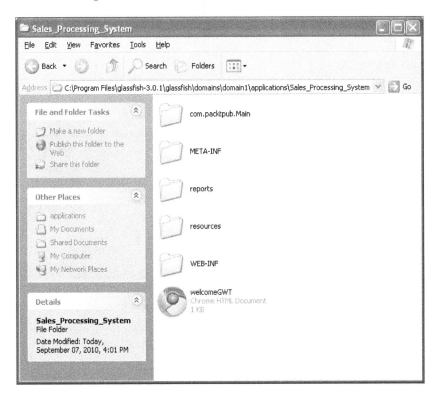

10
Using Speed Tracer

In this chapter, we will cover:

- ▸ Installing Speed Tracer
- ▸ Running Speed Tracer
- ▸ Analyzing event details
- ▸ Analyzing network (resources)
- ▸ Understanding hints

Introduction

Speed Tracer is a Google Chrome browser extension which is used to identify and fix performance problems in web applications. It visualizes metrics that are taken from low-level instrumentation points inside the browser, and analyzes them while the application is running. By using it, we are able to get a better picture of where time is being spent in the application.

Just for an example, Firebug is a similar tool, which is used in the Firefox browser.

Installing Speed Tracer

In this recipe, we are going to install Speed Tracer in the Google Chrome browser as an extension.

Getting ready

To install Speed Tracer, the Google Chrome browser needs to be started with a special tag, `--enable-extension-timeline-api` in order to enable Speed Tracer to work. To do this, we need to modify the Google Chrome shortcut as follows:

1. Right-click on the shortcut and select **Properties**.

2. Go to the **Target** field and paste `--enable-extension-timeline-api` at the end next to ...**chrome.exe"** after a space, as shown in the following screenshot:

3. Click on **Apply | OK**.

How to do it...

Now, carry out the following steps to install the extension:

1. Start the Google Chrome browser by clicking the modified shortcut.

2. Go to `http://code.google.com/webtoolkit/speedtracer/get-started.html#downloading`, and click on the **Install Speed Tracer (chrome extension)** button.

3. Install the downloaded extension.

How it works...

Speed Tracer is installed as an extension of the Google chrome browser. When the install is successful, a green stopwatch icon appears on the right-hand side of the browser's web address field. If this icon is clicked, the Speed Tracer Monitor window appears:

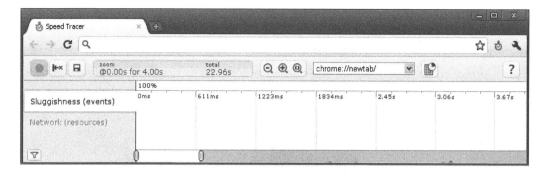

See also

▸ The *Running Speed Tracer* recipe

▸ The *Analyzing event details* recipe

▸ The *Analyzing network* recipe

▸ The *Understanding hints* recipe

Running Speed Tracer

In this recipe, we will run the Speed Tracer to analyze the page loading of our application.

Getting ready

Start the GlassFish Server and the Google Chrome browser with timeline API enabled.

How to do it...

1. Start the application by typing in the following URL in the address bar field:

    ```
    http://localhost:8080/Sales_Processing_System/
    ```

2. Click on the **Speed Tracer Monitor** icon.

3. **Refresh** the application window and see the monitor window, which looks as in the following screenshot:

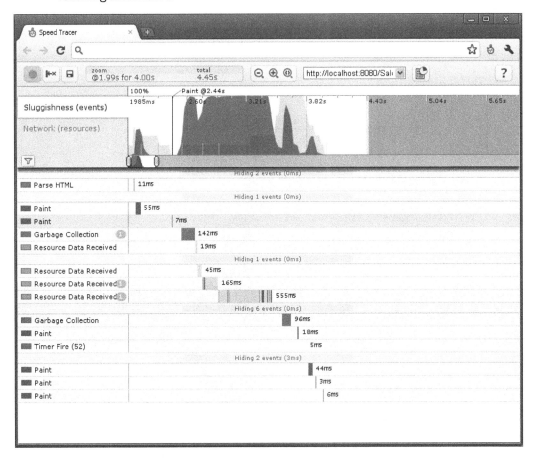

How it works...

Speed Tracer records the received data and show graphs for different aspects. From the graph, we can see the time for many browser events, some of which are as follows:

- **Parse HTML**
- **Paint**
- **Garbage Collection**
- **Resource Data Received**

There's more...

We can see the details for each browser event too, which is explained in the superseding recipes.

See also

- ▶ The *Installing Speed Tracer* recipe
- ▶ The *Analyzing event details* recipe
- ▶ The *Analyzing network* recipe
- ▶ The *Understanding hints* recipe

Analyzing event details

In this recipe, we are going to see the browser event details.

Getting ready

- ▶ Start the Google Chrome Browser with timeline API enabled
- ▶ Start the GlassFish Server
- ▶ Start the application
- ▶ Start the Speed Tracer monitor

How to do it...

1. Open the **Branch Form** and view the **Monitor** window:

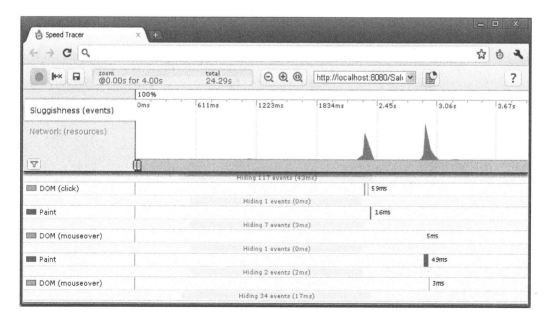

2. Click on the **DOM (click)** row at the bottom of the graph to see a detailed view of the click event, as shown in the following screenshot:

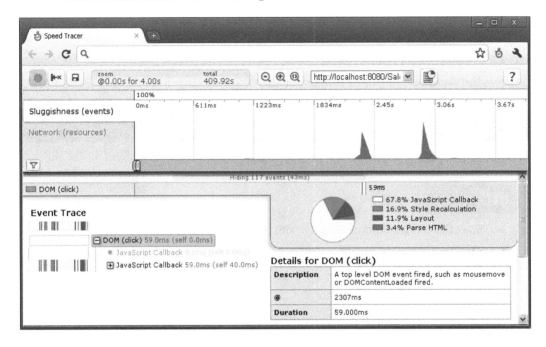

3. We have found the following details of the event, seen in the previous screenshot:

   □ **Description: A top level DOM event fired, such as mousemove or DOMContentLoaded fired**

   □ **Duration: 59.000ms**

   □ **Time Distribution: From the 59.000 ms, 67.8% time was spent for JasvaScript callback, 16.9 percent for style recalculation, 11.9% for layout; 3.4% for parse HTML**

4. In the same way, a detailed view can be seen for any other event.

See also

▶ The *Installing Speed Tracer* recipe

▶ The *Running Speed Tracer* recipe

▶ The *Analyzing network* recipe

▶ The *Understanding hints* recipe

Analyzing network

In this recipe, we are going to view the graph for the Network resource.

Getting ready

- ▸ Start the Google Chrome Browser with timeline API enabled
- ▸ Start the GlassFish Server
- ▸ Start the application
- ▸ Start the Speed Tracer monitor

How to do it...

1. **Refresh** the application window.
2. View the **Speed Tracer Monitor** window.
3. Go to the **Network (resources)** tab.

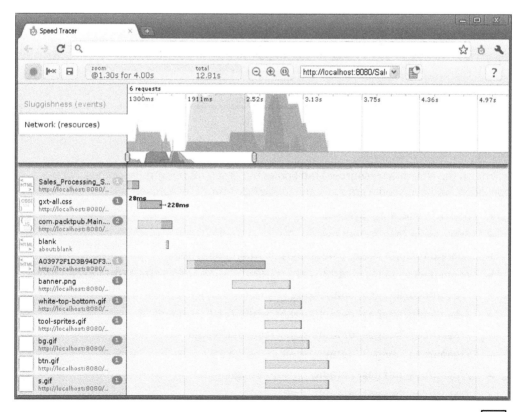

4. Click on **Sales_Processing_System** for a detailed view.

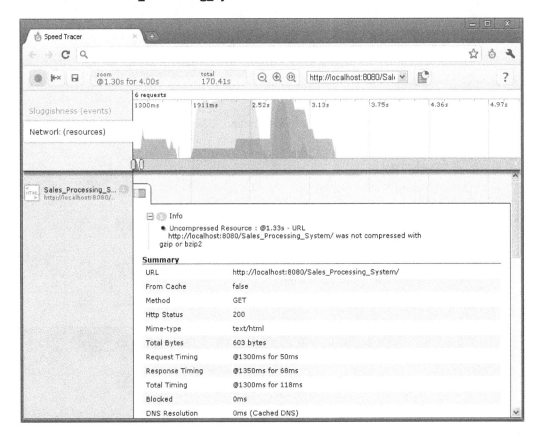

How it works...

Clicking on the **Network (resources)** tab shows the graph for network resources. For our application, we have seen a graph for the following network resources:

▸ **Sales_Processing_System**

▸ **/resources/css/gxt-all.css**

▸ **/com.packtpub.Main/com.packtpub.Main.nocache.js**

▸ **/com.packtpub.Main/A03972F1D3B94DF36F8AE92D4DAD7004.cache.html**

▸ **/resources/images/banner.png**

▸ **/resources/images/default/panel/white-top-bottom.gif**

▸ **/resources/images/default/panel/tool-sprites.gif**

▸ **/resources/images/default/toolbar/bg.gif**

▸ **/resources/images/default/button/btn.gif**

▸ **/resources/images/default/s.gif**

We can view the details for each of the above network resources. In the detailed view of the **Sales_Processing_System** resource, we have found the following data:

▸ Information with hints

▸ Summary that includes **URL**, **From Cache**, **Method**, **HTTP Status**, **Mime-type**, **Total Bytes**, **Request Timing**, **Response Timing**, and so on.

▸ Request headers that include **User-Agent**, **Accept**, and **Cache Control**.

▸ Response headers that include **Date**, **X-Powered-By**, **Content-Length**, **Last-Modified**, **Server**, **ETag**, **Content-Type**, and **Accept-Ranges**.

See also

▸ The *Installing Speed Tracer* recipe

▸ The *Running Speed Tracer* recipe

▸ The *Analyzing event details* recipe

▸ The *Understanding hints* recipe

Understanding hints

When we view the graphs for the Network resources, the Speed Tracer shows warning, hints for potential performance problems. Speed Tracer shows three types of hints in three colors based on the priority. The green color is for information or the lowest priority hint; warnings are shown in orange color and the critical highest priority hints are red-colored.

Getting ready

▸ Start the Google Chrome Browser with timeline API enabled

▸ Start the GlassFish Server

▸ Start the application

▸ Start the Speed Tracer monitor and go to the **Network (resources)** tab

How to do it...

When we see the graphs for **Network (resources)**, the hints are listed and counted for each resource. If there are warnings, some numbers (like **1** or **2**) are shown in oval shapes, which are colored according to the priority, as we see in the following screenshot:

Let's see the details of some hints. Clicking on the resource shows a detailed view of the hints. Click on the `http://localhost:8080/Sales_Processing_System/` resource on the left-hand side of the Speed Tracer window and see a detailed view, shown in the following screenshot:

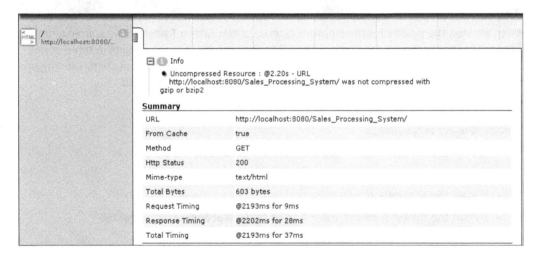

This hint is shown in green color, meaning that this is of a low priority. The message is an **Uncompressed Resource**.

Now let's see a warning. Click on **F3E0726D5C4489C97C5A8EA34F80AFDD.cache.html** and view the message:

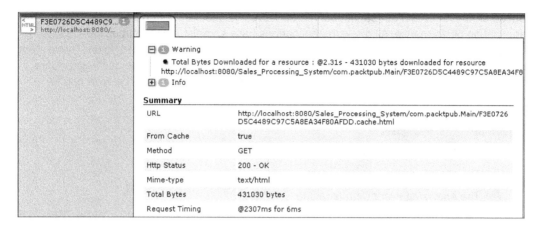

Here, the warning message is **Total Bytes Downloaded for a resource : @2.31s - 431030 bytes downloaded for resource**. This is shown as a warning because a large number of bytes are downloaded. In this case, we should know that the GWT application may load such a large resource at startup. Later, when the users experience the application, they get faster responses.

Now, we may look at a highest priority hint. Click on any resource with red color:

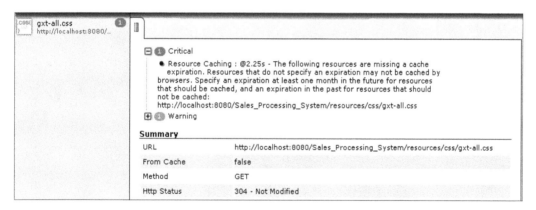

In our case, we have:

Resource Caching : @2.25s - The following resources are missing a cache expiration. Resources that do not specify an expiration may not be cached by browsers. Specify an expiration at least one month in the future for resources that should be cached, and an expiration in the past for resources that should not be cached:

http://localhost:8080/Sales_Processing_System/resources/css/gxt-all.css

Based on the hints and our application perspective, we should work on improving the application performance. All the web applications have some static resources like CSS, images, and so on, which never change, such as logo, navigation bars, and so on. These static resources can be cached in the browser cache of the client PC. Client-side caching reduces the server load, as the cached resources can be loaded directly from the browser cache.

See also

▸ The *Installing Speed Tracer* recipe

▸ The *Running Speed Tracer* recipe

▸ The *Analyzing event details* recipe

Index

U

user
  authenticating, by login process 154, 155
UsersDTO object 155
UsersJpaController class 155

V

variables
  adding 177-180
VerticalPanel class
  about 50

alignment, setting for 50

W

WAR file
  creating 196
  deploying, in GlassFish Server 210, 211
Web Application Archive file. *See* **WAR file**
WHERE clause 168
widgets
  about 53
  using, in form 54

About Packt Publishing

Packt, pronounced 'packed', published its first book "*Mastering phpMyAdmin for Effective MySQL Management*" in April 2004 and subsequently continued to specialize in publishing highly focused books on specific technologies and solutions.

Our books and publications share the experiences of your fellow IT professionals in adapting and customizing today's systems, applications, and frameworks. Our solution based books give you the knowledge and power to customize the software and technologies you're using to get the job done. Packt books are more specific and less general than the IT books you have seen in the past. Our unique business model allows us to bring you more focused information, giving you more of what you need to know, and less of what you don't.

Packt is a modern, yet unique publishing company, which focuses on producing quality, cutting-edge books for communities of developers, administrators, and newbies alike. For more information, please visit our website: www.packtpub.com.

About Packt Open Source

In 2010, Packt launched two new brands, Packt Open Source and Packt Enterprise, in order to continue its focus on specialization. This book is part of the Packt Open Source brand, home to books published on software built around Open Source licences, and offering information to anybody from advanced developers to budding web designers. The Open Source brand also runs Packt's Open Source Royalty Scheme, by which Packt gives a royalty to each Open Source project about whose software a book is sold.

Writing for Packt

We welcome all inquiries from people who are interested in authoring. Book proposals should be sent to author@packtpub.com. If your book idea is still at an early stage and you would like to discuss it first before writing a formal book proposal, contact us; one of our commissioning editors will get in touch with you.

We're not just looking for published authors; if you have strong technical skills but no writing experience, our experienced editors can help you develop a writing career, or simply get some additional reward for your expertise.